LIFE AND ADVENTURES OF

RED CROW

FORMERLY HEAD CHIEF
OF THE BLOODS

by Red Crow

(c. 1830 – 28 August 1900)

Originally published
1891

I was born at Fort Whoop-up about the year 1830. My father's name was "Black Bear" and my Mother's was "Handsome Woman." My male parent was a great chief. I only knew two of his wives, my Mother and another. I had three half-brothers, who were not my Mother's children. I lost them all in the days of the smallpox, they all then being single at their death.

I also had two Sisters but they too are long since dead and none of their children are alive now. The well-known Blood Chief "Far Seer" was my Uncle, for he was a younger Brother of my Father's. My baby name was "Captured the gun inside," this name was given me in memory of an event in the life of my grandfather. When I first took the war-trail my name was changed to "Lately Tom" which name I greatly disliked and did my best to throw off and repudiate, but in spite of my known disgust bore the name for many years until I became known as "Red Crow," the former name of an old relative. When I returned from my visit to Eastern Canada in 1865 I acquired my present and fourth name ("Sitting White Buffalo").

My first war path was with a large party against the "Cree." I did not capture anything, but many of the elder men did so and returned home at once on their new horses, leaving us unsuccessful ones to make the best of our way home, on foot, this being the custom.

Next summer I made another attempt and was a little more fortunate for although I captured nothing, I was presented with a horse by one who did, a relation of mine in the party. This last expedition was a very large one under the leadership of "Middle Painted Lodge," the old man who died last summer.

As soon as we returned home from that trip, off I went with a party under "Red Old Man" of our band. His party was not numerous and the Crow were the enemy. Upon this, my third war path, I captured two animals, a buckskin mare and a pinto gelding.

Next summer after that I joined an immense party of Bloods, Sarcees, Blackfeet under the Chief of the latter tribe, "Sun Old Man" (Old Sun), this party was mounted and our direction was North to the

Cree Country. We started from camp on the Red Deer and away off near the Saskatchewan we sighted three Cree hunters. Knowing well that they would run at sight of our large party, we hid ourselves in low ground and some of our men turned the hair side of their robes outwards and then went out on foot on a hill nearby and then imitated the actions of buffalo. This trick succeeded, for the Cree hunters came for them and ran into the ambush, so out we all rushed and killed them easily, but not before one of our men got a bullet in his shoulder end another, "Big Plume," a stab in the back with a broad dagger. Two of the Crees were armed with guns, which were captured by Bloods.

A Blackfoot took the weapons of the other Cree which were a bow and arrows. I contented myself with capturing a white blanket, (one then very valuable) and relieved one of the dead Crees of his scalp. Upon our return to camp I became one of a small dismounted party that was about to start to the Crows under "Morning Paper." This party was so small that we only required one brush lodge at nights, (about 8 or 10).

Upon our arrival in the country of the Crows we, one moonlight night, approached a camp of these people. I succeeded in getting three horses which I led some little distance from, the camp and tied them up in a clump of bush. Noting the place I returned, to endeavor to obtain more, but before I could do so the whole affair was bungled by a Blackfoot of our party in this way: One of the Crow Indians had a valuable horse probably a racer which was standing in a lodge, the front of which had been unlaced and spread out for that purpose. Our friend the Blackfoot saw this animal, and, knowing that none but a good horse would be cared for in that way, he desired very much to ride that horse home to the Blackfoot camp. No sooner did this desire possess him than he attempted to carry it out, for the fearless fellow at once jumped on the horse's back thinking to cut him loose and ride him boldly out of camp. But the Crows were not to be deprived so easily of their favorite steed, for up in front of the horse sprung a Crow with gun in hand and our Blackfoot being as nimble as he was reckless, slipped off and escaped to the friendly bushes, with only a bullet hole in his robe. Of course the firing of that shot alarmed the Crow village and all was confusion in an instant. I was at that time in another part of the camp quietly looking for some horse to lead out, and now left as fast as I could run, but could not get to the animals I had tied in the timber for the Crows were out and I had to leave the locality at once. Away out on the hills I came across first one, then 3 others, of our party some of whom had taken many horses, we then started for home, our other companions had scattered from the Crow camp and gone home by other routes.

Upon our way Northward we four met a war party of Crows, chased and fought them to no purpose in a running contest in which no one was hurt. We arrived home without other adventures and found our missing friends there before us.

Three days only did I remain at home, when I left again for the same country with a party led by "Red Old Man."

Away down in that Southern country we struck a trail of a camp of Snakes and myself and four others followed it, the remainder of our party went on in another direction. Before we had gone far we found three horses and tried to catch them, but they were fat and wild and would not let us near them but ran over a hill and continued grazing. I noted the place and continued upon the trail of the Snake camp and in two days overtook it and saw that it was a large village. But they were taking down lodges and preparing to move when we found then, so we were soon in possession of the vacated camp-ground, near which we found a stray horse. As he might come in handy we caught him and led him along with us, following again the fresh trail of the Snake Indians, which led away over the mountains. The cayuse we used to scout with. One of us would ride him on ahead of the other two. When the Snakes camped again, we were close behind, and at night I was told to go and make the first effort to take horses. I went alone and in the darkness caught an unbroken colt in mistake. The wild brute stampeded to the camp with me, I hung on to my rope and was dragged close to the village, so close that my heart was away up in my throat when to my great relief the animal dropped, choked by my noose around his neck. I quickly unfastened my rope and got away without disturbing the sleeping Indians. I now cut off a small bunch from the large herd that was grazing some distance from the lodges. These I quietly drove away as rapidly as I could on foot. Before I had gone far I heard an Indian come out from one of the lodges and round up all the rest of the horses and drive them in between lodges to the space in the middle of the camp. He had not noticed anything and was not giving any alarm, but was doing what Indians often did in those days for safety. As he drove the herd through the camp he kept shouting out something. I guessed that he was telling the people that they should hobble and picket more of their animals at night so that the herd would not stray so far from the village. I soon had my little herd of horses a safe distance away, so caught and mounted one and went to find my four companions. They were not where I had left them, so thinking that they had mistaken the shouting of the noisy Snake Indian for an alarm and had stampeded in consequence, I struck off at a run to find then, taking a course that I thought might intercept them. On the top of a ridge I saw the head of a coulee which I started to ride down, and in the darkness ahead of me heard voices. Upon approaching the speakers I recognised my friend's voices and heard one say "here comes a rider," at which they all scampered off, followed at a gallop and as the hostile village was far out of earshot I shouted and stopped them. After explanations I guided them to where my horses were, which upon counting we found to number about 40.

I told them to help themselves end divide up the band between them, I reserving one fine horse for my own use. We at once began our retreat homewards, but our good luck was only of short duration, for when driving along at a fast pace a flock of grouse flew up in front of our horses and frightened them to such an extent that they stampeded in the wildest disorder and were soon lost in the darkness. It being still a long time before daylight I proposed to return and make another trial at the village but my comrades would not hear of it, and a long argument resulted in I and one companion returning to make an attempt to recover the lost horses or capture other ones. We gave our mounts to our friends and went back afoot, but before parting we named a place where we would overtake them should we be successful. When we reached the camp again we saw that our band of horses had returned to the main herd within the circle, so we crossed the river between the village and went around to the opposite side, thinking to enter from that direction and lead or drive horses from the herd. But we stumbled against a guard who was warming himself by a small fire in a little brush shelter and we beat a retreat from his locality without being seen.

I proposed to my friend to take a trip out in the plain on that side and should there be no animals grazing there to the centre of the camp we would go. He agreed to this and we separated to search the prairie. I found three, one ran away to camp, but a mare I caught, although she nearly dragged me into the village before I could get her bridled; the third horse was her foal so when I mounted and rode off, he followed. I found my comrade, who got up behind me, and we continued our search. We were rewarded with 9 more horses one of which was a big brown, a fine animal with eagle feathers tied in his mane end a rope on one foot. This one I mounted, turning loose the mare and as soon as my friend had mounted also, we drove away our captures and kept on all that night and the next day in the direction our friends had gone.

It was near sundown when we approached the place where our companions were to wait for us, and were glad to find that a glass was flashing at us from a bunch of pine timber nearby. This we knew to be our three men whom we soon rejoined and, just as the sun went out of sight, we divided up the horses and began preparations to continue our flight Northward. We were soon on the way again and rode that night until Just before daylight when we reached the first place of safety, and were able to have the sleep which we so much needed. Before the Sun was high next day we mounted again and continued the retreat; that day we found a place where a fire had been made, and some cooking had been done. There was also a place where people had passed the night. After closely examining the signs we saw that it had been the camp of our main party. Upon making this discovery we took up their trail and next day we came in sight of them as they were starting out in their days work, for they had been unsuccessful and were going home on foot, we were far behind them, so that they did not see us at first. A Blackfoot was bringing up their rear and he was some long distance behind the one next to him; thinking to scare him, we quietly rode along behind him until when quite close we suddenly began to sing and made for him. He did not turn to see who we were but simply went at the greatest speed his legs were capable of, to our great amusement. We dismounted and drove our horses ahead, not caring to ride and leave the others when we came near to the place where we had seen the three wild horses on our road South, I and my chum mounted and went and found and drove them in; they were a valuable addition to our stock of horses, for they were fat and good. During the same day a heavy rain-storm came upon us but we could not afford to camp and went on through the mud and wet. Travelling in this state we came to a river which we crossed and one of the men ascended the bank on that side to look about, although the rain was falling so thickly that we could not see far. The scout had no sooner arrived at the top of the hill than he came running down to us and informed us that we were in the immediate vicinity of a large camp of Indians which was situated on the same river just below where we stood. We mounted and quietly went up the river bottom to a safe distance where we halted and I proposed that we should all go down and get some horses under cover of the heavy rain. My companions would not agree to this, the elder ones said that the risk was too great in broad daylight. They argued that the storm might clear away at any moment, and the people in the camp, whoever they were, would then be able to see us at their horses. The idea was too dangerous to consider, they all said, but I was determined to try once so I set out alone. My chum, "Big Plume," ran after me with the intention of persuading me to turn from my purpose, but I persuaded him instead and he came with me on my errand. Our party took their departure at the same time as we did. I and "Big Plume" soon were close to the strange village which we found to be of the "Nez Perce" tribe with whom we were at war. As soon as we were satisfied on that point we turned our attention to their horses, I threw my rope at a buckskin but missed, and caught a bald faced bay instead which turned out to be a good fast animal. "Big Plume," having now also roped a likely looking horse, we mounted and left the locality, being satisfied with one each under such dangerous circumstances. It was considered a rather clever feat, to go close to a hostile camp and capture horses in daylight. We overtook the others and our success tempted the leader, "Red Old Man," upon remaining with most of the men to take Nez Perce horses. My four successful friends and I started to go home but I became separated from them in this manner. One day, passing near some buffalo, I went over to kill one, leaving the four men to wait for me near by. When about to fire I noticed a large number of buffalo running towards me from over the nearest ridge and upon hearing gunshots in that direction I Immediately turned loose my horse and got in cover, for I thought that the herd was being run by Indians who in that country were likely to be hostile. Presently a mounted Indian came over the ridge running a buffalo which he killed not far from my hiding place.

A squaw and a boy joined the man, and they skinned and cut up the beast and took away the meat. When they were safely out of sight, I left my cover and went to examine the carcass. By the way it was skinned I at once saw that the butcher was one of our nation. I ran after the hunter and was seen by him, who returned and approached me. He was a South Piegan and I mounted behind him and he took me to his camp, but not before I discovered that my four companions had deserted me, no doubt they stampeded at the sound of the Piegan's gun. I remained with the Piegan's family one night, leaving the next night for the North. That place was on White River. The Piegans were camped all along the stream in groups of two or four lodges etc., hunting buffalo. After travelling eight days I arrived at Fort Benton and there found my friends with my horses. I gave one horse to Mr. Culbertson and received some tobacco and other goods. Not approving of the way in which my four comrades had left me, I parted company with them by taking my horses and starting for home alone. I found a camp of Blackfeet on Milk River and was directed by them to some Bloods, my relations, whose lodges were pitched lower down on the same stream. While resting at that Blood camp, the other four of my late companions turned up and with them I went over to the Cut Bank to visit some Piegan friends. My horses, seven in number, I left with my Blood relatives as I wished them to fatten up. After remaining there a few days we came on home.

When I set out upon my next trip it was from my home on the Kootenai, for my uncle's lodge was pitched on that stream near the "big stone," the main lodge of our tribe being away, hunting in the south. I led this party myself, my followers were four in number only, and our object was as usual to take horses from the Crows. It was in the fall of the year and we went to the Bears River and followed it down to the Missouri. Here I had a dream, I dreamt that at a place I knew well the, "big hill," there was a large herd of horses, and after telling my dream to my friends we set out to find them. In going towards the "Big Butte" we discovered a large camp of the Crows.

I went in alone and took a gray mare, we all went up in to some pine timber on a hill and made there our little brush camp.

Three nights we laid low, then I visited the Crows again and brought back two animals, a black stallion and a pinto. Four more nights we remained in camp then all of us went to see our neighbours, but we only succeeded in capturing two horses, one of which was taken by me. Having now horses for all of our party, we left that place and went to the "Big Butte" and we ascended to look about, from there I saw the identical big herd of horses that had dreamed about. We descended and went in the direction of the horses, but to reach them it was necessary to cross a river which was covered with slippery ice. While busy carrying dirt, making a path on the ice upon which our horses could walk, a large party of Blackfeet came along and joined our party. A few of them being on foot crossed the river without any trouble and went ahead and stole a great number of horses from the big herd we were after. I and the others finally crossed and in approaching the balance of the coveted horses I came across one of their owners and was just about to shoot him when I discovered to my surprise that he was a Blood. He informed me that he was one of a party of Bloods and Piegans who had taken the big herd of horses from the Crows and that he was now looking for more than half of them which had lately disappeared. I explained that mystery by telling him that some of the Blackfeet of my party had relieved him of his horses and that they were now on their road north with them.

Our party now split up, five went back to the Crow camp we had just left, some went home with the lucky Bloods and Piegans and I took the opportunity to send back my four horses by a young man to whom I gave one of them for the trouble of delivering the other three at the Blood camp. One horse I sent to my uncle, one to a female relative, and the other I sent to the woman who had supplied me with moccasins when I left home on this trip. I also sent a message to my relatives to the effect that, when I had captured many horses I would return home and not before, even should it take me until the next summer to do so. Five of us started out on a new expedition and were soon joined by 12 more making a good party of 17. For many days and nights I slept and fasted by myself, seeking for an indication as to what to do the night at last I received the sign. I dreamt that at a certain mountain were a great number of horses. We at once went there and found the dream to be true, for in the neighborhood was a large village of Snake Indians, their horses grazing in every direction around the camp. The first night I captured 6 and sent them home by two young fellows. Ten of our men went away to see what they could do, and I and one other went again for horses. Eleven remained in camp to await our return. I was not unsuccessful this time, for I returned with a large herd, as many as I could drive. Upon my reaching camp I found only five of the party waiting for us, two had gone away in one direction, and another party of four, all Blackfeet, had gone out to get horses, the former soon returned but not the four. One of the five who were waiting for us was "Eagle Ribs," my friend and a chief afterwards. I said to him, "take your choice of all these horses my friend, for you are a married man and I am single."

When he had done so I picked out two only and told the people to help themselves, to divide up the band amongst them. For our Northern home we now started, and one day, I being on the lead saw some horses hobbled, there was no doubt a camp near by. Of these I took 4 making in all 6, which I kept and brought home safely with one exception, a black which played out. We made Quick time out of that country for we kept up a fast pace for 3 days and 4 nights without any sleep to amount to anything, nor food. On our way we found a late camp-ground of the Snakes, so fresh was it that the fire-places were still warm, but we had had enough and were anxious to see our people so pressed on. At the Red Deer we saw a large village, which we avoided and circled, but our trail was discovered and followed by a numerous party who would have overtaken us had not a blizzard struck us, and in that friendly storm we made our escape without even losing our horses. At the South Piegan camp I found my uncle who, with my other relations, had moved there during my absence. We were all very much played out and ragged when we arrived home. It was Springtime, the ducks had arrived ahead of us. Nothing was ever heard of those four Blackfeet, from that day to this, and, I often wonder if they are wandering about in that distant country yet.

One night only did I remain at home. A large war-party was about to start to the Crow country again under the guidance of "Red Old Man" and I could not resist the desire for more adventure, so I at once prepared and went with them. Early one morning I was out scouting after we had reached the hostile country, and from a hill I saw away in the distance some buffalo running and, hearing a faint sound of gun shots in the same direction, I rejoined my friends and communicated to them the news that we were in the locality of our enemies. Large parties like this were in the habit of travelling in the daytime and resting at night, for many scouts would be thrown out in front and at each side so that there was not much risk of being seen. Good experienced men were generally chosen, for that work. We at once painted up and prepared for battle, and set out to find the hunters whom we soon discovered busy skinning the animals they had killed. We approached them without showing ourselves and on one of their horses, (of which they had five) was a Gros Ventre saddle. We, judging from the saddle that the people were Gros Ventres and friends, left our cover and went towards then, at which they fled in haste towards a hill. The five horses scampered off also, their owners not having time to mount. Over the hill disappeared the fleeing Indians, we in hot pursuit.

Before we reached the hill, however, to our great surprise and discomfort, a great crowd of people appeared upon it coming towards us. Seeing at a glance that we were vastly outnumbered, we turned and ran away at our best speed. Looking back we saw to our consternation that the prairie behind us was black with people, a great many of them mounted and coming for us yelling like fiends. They soon overtook the hindmost of our men, and killed the two Bloods and a Piegan. Another of our party was about to suffer the same fate but we heard him appealing to us for help, so we ran back and rescued him. Here we made a stand, and a fight followed in which Red Old Man was shot through the thigh. The Snakes were, it seems, satisfied with having killed three of us without losing any of their own number, for they now withdrew and went home in great glee. We made a bier with willows and robes upon which we laid our leader and carried him away homewards. Six men at a time would carry the wounded chief, with frequent shifts we were able to do fairly good travelling. At "Snow Mountain," we left Red Old Man with one attendant and pushed on so that we could more quickly send him assistance and horses to bring him home. We had not gone far, however, before we met a very large party of Piegans. It was a war party with women and lodges. Some of them went away to the main camp of the Piegans to send, as I said, help to "Red Old Man."

The rest, with ourselves, turned in the direction of the Snake village. Being now so strongly reinforced, we were anxious to have satisfaction for our late defeat. When we discovered our enemies again they were on the move and I, with field glass, followed and watched them all day and saw when they camped at night. I guided our men to the spot, but when we approached the camp-fires, we discovered that the people had fled. They had made a night move thinking to evade any possible pursuers, and had left fires burning. We now scattered our men all over the surrounding country in search of the fugitive camp, it became too dark to see the trail. At last the searchers located the Snake village, neatly hidden on a creek, a branch of the stream it had been pitched on before. We captured an immense band of their horses and did it in such a bold style that we were seen, and the owners turned out in force to retake them. When they saw how strong we were in numbers they gave up the task, but not before one of their foremost braves had fallen a victim to our weapons. He was killed by a Piegan. We were thus able to go home with blackened faces.

My chum "Big Plume" and I went away by ourselves from home at the Piegan village, our destination was the Crows. The day after we started we were overtaken by a number of young men who were determined to go with us. One day while scouting I saw a prairie fire start up. I went to high ground overlooking that vicinity and discovered a moving camp of Indians. I kept them within sight and noted where they camped, then returned to bring along my party. That night the moon was at the full and when we approached the hostile camps we found they had all their horses in the middle. While waiting and considering what we could do under the circumstances, I saw three bay horses stray out of camp. When they were out a little distance I caught two of them and my chum took the other. We led the horses away across the river and tied them in the timber, then returned to attempt to capture some more. Presently five more animals came straying out and as we went to catch them, up jumped a great crowd of armed Indians from the cover all about us. They had been doubtless lying in ambush for us all night and were turning these horses loose as a bait, in the midst of a storm of missiles we managed to reach the river and crossed to the other side. We had fortunately tied our five horses a long way from the village so that we were now able to reach them and were soon mounted and away in safety. Our Piegan companions were not to be found; they had stampeded at the firing in the camp so we went home alone, arriving as the Sun dance was about to take place.

Under the guidance of the Blackfeet Chief "Big Snake" a party started out, of which I was a member, the destination and object again were Crows and Crow horses. Our trip Southwards was made without any events worth relating. We were not long in finding a village of the owners of the much coveted horses, but they were too much on the alert, so, finding from the position and appearance of camp that they were apparently expecting an attempt upon their stock, we drew off and went in search of other villages. Not being at all successful, we were returning to the locality of this Crow camp when early one morning, just after we had butchered a two-year-old buffalo, we were attacked by a large number of our enemies. During the scrimmage which ensued we lost four of our men, whose bodies of course fell into the hands of the Crows as we were retreating in search of a suitable position to make a stand and defend ourselves.

We reached a hollow in the hills and there fought for some hours. Here someone of us killed a Crow from off his horse, a black which we caught, and I mounted and left my companions to search for a better location. Our enemies were being constantly reinforced and we knew that unless we gained a very strong position we would have little chance of surviving. I dashed out on the black horse and galloped here and there looking for a suitable nook. At last I found a natural fort and rode into it to Inspect it; the Crows saw me and some of then made a rush at me, but I returned unhurt to where my friends were. I had some difficulty in persuading them to leave their hollow to occupy the other, on account of the risk in exposing themselves to the fire of the Crows, while doing so. Finally they all agreed and we made a break, I leading on the Crow stud.

Our movement was so quickly made, and so unexpected by our enemies, that we all reached the point in safety, with the exception of one man who became separated from the rest and hid himself in a crevice of the rocks some little distance away. We were no sooner in our new hole, which proved to be a perfect stronghold, than the Crows closed in upon us, to so short a distance that our separated companion could not reach us without making himself a target for a hundred weapons. Fortunately for him, however, the Crows did not notice where he went to, and he was not molested, but remained out of sight all day amusing himself by singing etc. All that long Summer's day the battle lasted. The Crows made four great charges upon our position but were each time driven back with heavy losses. They came so close to us that we seldom missed a shot. Had they been half as careful we would not have seen the Sunrise very high that day. At one time our foe came within ten feet of us, and I sprang up on our rocky breastwork drew my bow in a threatening manner at which the foremost retreated. It was always with great risk that we showed our persons to them. Some of their men had moved a lot of stones to the top of a little hill nearby, and from behind them they would fire a volley every time they saw one of our heads. A Crow called out in the Blackfeet language, enquiring who we were, I replied that I was a Blood. He assured me that not one of us would live to tell the story of this fight, for said he, "we have you securely and you cannot escape." We laughed at this and taunted them to do their best, telling them that they could not hurt us, though they were as numerous as trees.

The 4th charge was made a little before sundown and as before none of us were hit. Our position was almost entirely surrounded by big stones and rocks, with some fir trees offering us admirable cover and making it impossible for a number of horsemen to ride in upon us. During these charges it was very exciting work for us, no sound could be heard but gun shots end yells; the Crows calling to each other to have courage and not retreat and we shouting our yells of defiance. At sundown they all drew off and we could see them having a talk, after which there was singing, dancing and more preparations made for war. We, at this, thought that another charge was intended but they had a different scheme. A circle of fires were made around us, the crafty fellows were not going to let us steal away in the darkness, the one who spoke our language, again called out, with the pleasant intelligence that they were going to starve us out, because among the men killed was a great chief, a young man, who must be avenged. Our reply was as before, "do your best, you are quite harmless and we have no fear of being hurt." In truth, thirst was the only thing that was bothering us. As soon as it was dark, our man in the crevice made his escape and we saw no more of him.

Several times we attempted to get away; one of the men would remain in the fort and keep a mock conversation with himself to make our foes think that we were all there yet, then we would all crawl out and try to pass between the fires for the Crows were not in sight. We were driven back each time, they had us so completely hemmed in that a hundred seemed to spring up in front of us no matter what direction we started for. After half of the night had passed in this manner, I thought of an old trick and decided to give it a try. I set fire to a big pine tree which made a very dense black smoke. The prevailing breeze kept the smoke down in a large black cloud close to the ground. We at once took our departure and keeping well in the smoke, I leading, we all crawled past our watchful enemies the Crows and reached the bushes unseen. I expect they watched our burning tree a long time before they guessed its use. We arrived in safety at our main camp which was at "Bear Paw Mountain," and heard that the other man had come some time before us and had told in what a plight he had left us. The chiefs had decided to wait 4 days for us, they said that no besieged party could hold out more than 3 days without water and little ammunition. But during those three days we were coming home and arrived on the 4th. The people were very angry with "Big Snake" for making such a bungle of the expedition. All the chiefs accused him of cowardness and bad judgement, his life was even threatened, while I was given much praise for having saved the lives of the party. My coat was full of bullet and arrow holes as were also the garments of many of the others. The first time after the escape that I unbraided my hair, a big lock of it came loose in my hand, it had been cut off by a Crow bullet. You can judge how busy we were defending ourselves when I did not notice that bullet.

This camp at "Bear Paw" was a very large affair, the lodges of almost all of our nation being pitched there. I was not permitted to remain and rest myself for "Big Snake" was very much ashamed of himself and asked me to go with him again on the war-path in order that he might redeem his lost honor. He pressed me to accompany him, so one night we quietly left camp alone. Next morning, as soon as it became known throughout the camp that we two were missing, a crowd of about 50 young men from the 4 tribes, packed up and followed us. They overtook us that day, all declared that they would come, and "Big Snake" was the leader of a strong party of Piegans, Bloods, Blackfeet and Gros Ventres. On a hill called the Owl Head we were resting one day at noon, having ascended to the top for that purpose, and to view the surrounding country. The whole district was black with buffalo, while I was engaged in surveying the scene through my glass, my attention was drawn to a commotion amongst the animals on the distant hills. I looked closely and plainly saw two riders running a buffalo which soon fell. I told my comrades who took the glass and looked but none of them could see anything. Their eyes were not used to the instrument therefore I could see better with it than they. A Gros Ventre called "The Fox" volunteered to go and scout; with him went three others, a Piegan, a Blood and a Blackfoot, they returned and at once accused me of lying to them; they said that there was not a sign in the locality I had mentioned. I made no remark but became determined to find the man who killed the buffalo and prove my truthfulness. An animal was now butchered and all were soon busy making brush lodges and otherwise preparing to camp. I was sitting with some others on the hill and saw a wounded buffalo passing in sight. I rid myself of my companions by saying that I was going over to kill it and that they had better go to camp.

As soon as I was out of their sight I changed my course and ran in a straight line to the point where I had seen the hunters at noon. I reached the spot and was not at all surprised when there I saw the carcass of a newly killed bull from which ran away a pack of coyotes at my approach. When I quit my comrades I did not bring my rope, because taking it would cause them to suspect my errand. Having now found the carcass I would be helpless in my next step, unless I provided myself with a rope. With my knife I began cutting from the shoulder of the dead buffalo, the long hair which grows there and which can be easily braided into a fairly serviceable lariat. While engaged at this work

I heard a noise like the panting of a running man, and after peering into the darkness for some time, I thought I could discern something passing near me, so I called several times in a low voice, "Come here! Come here!" at which the something came cautiously towards me and proved to be "Big Snake," who had missed me and guessing my motive he had followed to share my adventures. "Look at this carcass," said I, "this is what caused me to be called a liar." We now ran away through the darkness to find the camp of the hunters, stopping every little While to   listen attentively for sounds to guide us. Again and again we sped through the night, again and again we listened, when at last a most welcome sound reached our straining ears, it was the deep beating of a tom-tom.

"What did I tell you," cried I to my companion, "I lied did I?" "Big Snake" asked me to take the lead in what work was before us. He said that so many people at home had wished him bad luck and abused him that he no longer had faith in his medicine. He knew that my medicine was strong and that it would be better for us both for me to lead, which I did. Guided by the sound of the drum we soon discovered a large camp of Indians who were dancing and singing in many of the lodges. In a coulee we got five horses, I gave "Big Snake" three, he being a married man; the two best I reserved for myself.

We each mounted a horse, after hobbling the rest. Continuing the circle we found three more and drove them to the first three. "Big Snake" proposed that we content ourselves with what we had and go, to which I agreed. Not feeling well disposed towards those who had accused me of falsehood, I thought that I would pay them out, so we went straight home without going near them.

"Big Snake" carried on this trip one of the Medicine Pipes, known as "the Black Covers," and on our return during the first day he offered it to me for the big bay horse I rode, I accepted the pipe and transferred it to my back. We afterwards found some more horses and he preferred one of them to the others I had given him, so I allowed him it and retained the bay. My companion on the last day before reaching home kept driving his horses ahead by himself because they were more easily driven than mine, which gave me very much trouble. They were continually running back in the direction of their old home. I nearly played out my horse in driving them against their will. I got off the tired animal I was riding and leading him I walked ahead to where "Big Snake" was waiting for us, the 7 horses I left behind where I had dismounted. I was very angry when I met my comrade and said to him, "Here take back your sacred pipe I do not want it. I have on this trip given you 4 horses and thought that you would help me drive mine; the animal I gave you is back with my horses, go and get him and give me the one you ride." He refused the pipe and promised to help me but I was very much displeased with him and made him take it back.

We continued our homeward travels and the same day, he now assisting me, we crossed the Missouri. Near Bear Paw I ascended a high hill and from there I saw three people through my glass, and made them out to be a war-party of Crees, knowing them to be of that tribe by their dress and manner. I signalled to my partner, who came up and agreed with me that they were three Crees. We went down out of sight of the others and cached our horses, all but the two we rode, in the brush. Our plan was to ambush the unsuspecting Crees. We noticed that they were following at that time a buffalo trail and we posted ourselves in the bush at a point where their trail crossed a little coulee. Here we watched them coming straight towards us. Our two horses were standing at the bottom of the coulee and the lariat of mine was in my hand, so that I could quickly mount and be off should it be necessary. "Big Snake" had tied his horse to a tree but now went to untie him. I had grass and sage brush tied to my head to prevent our enemies seeing me until very close, then it would be too late, for our intention was to kill two of them at first fire. I had said to "Big Snake," "if I kill, you take the arms, and if you kill I will take the arms." As I watched the approaching Crees, they were almost to us, I turned to see what was keeping my companion. It was time to act. I did not see him at the moment and upon looking again to the front, what was my surprise to see the three intended victims fleeing in the opposite direction as fast as their limbs could carry them. The clumsy Blackfoot, in returning to me from his horse, had popped up his head to the view of the Crees, who saw him and were off. I was on my horse in an instant and after them. They were running for a clump of timber and I put my horse to his best speed in order to cut them off. The distance was too short, for the fleeing trio, throwing their bundles and blankets away as they ran, reached the edge of the timber and after firing at me they disappeared into cover. I looked behind expecting to find "Big Snake" at my heels, but the lazy fellow was just emerging from our late ambush and was starting his horse into a lazy lope. So the three Crees escaped that day.

We arrived home without further events, being only absent 8 days, five of which were spent in going down, and in our return. I gathered up the thrown-away goods of the Crees and gave them to "Big Snake" a Hudson Bay striped Blanket coat, moccasins and a rope. The medicine pipe I referred to was of the black covered sort, it was given to "Big Snake" by the men who made it, a Blackfoot called "Many Knees," they are carried on the war-path to use in changing the weather. Big Snake was very anxious that I should sell him my "medicine", but I had no confidence in his courage, so I refused.

On the Red Deer were pitched the lodges of the Bloods, Blackfoot, Piegans, and Sarcees. The latter tribe had lately suffered rather severely in war with the Crees, a favorite chief and many others had fallen. On an errand of revenge a large, very large party was organized under the Blood "Bull shakes his tent." We set out, all mounted, and travelling Northwards and at a place called "Round Bushes" or "Round Timbers" we saw a distant Cree camp. Some of our wild young men wanted to ride boldly to it and attack it, but we wiser ones told them that they would certainly be killed if they did that, for the distance was so great that they would be overtaken if pursued before they could return to us. Some of the unruly young fellows attempted several times to go in spite of our advice, but I headed them off and made them wait and listen to reason. One of the chiefs called our attention to a road by which we could all ride almost unseen to within a short distance of our enemies' camp. We covered the fronts of our light coloured horses with buffalo robes and made the party look like buffalo and walked our horses towards a certain hill that was between us and the camp. Several times we had to take to open prairie, but walked slow like buffalo and all lowered our heads and horses' necks, and reached the hill, behind which all of us painted and made ready for action. I crawled to the top of the hill, leading my horse, and saw the Cree men away running buffalo. Near us and between us and the camp were ten people who had been getting water and were now on their way back to the village.

I signalled to the men and continued watching the water-carriers. There were two women on ahead then six women and a mounted man, and a single woman bringing up the rear, 9 squaws and one man, all loaded with water kegs. As soon as I saw our party behind the hill mounting, I sprang on my horse, and started down the opposite slope after the squaws. I had a good start of any of our party and was soon close behind the water carriers, who had heard nothing and were slowly plodding along. Soon, however, our big party came around the hill and in sight, and as they broke into a run, all yelling, the squaws looked behind. Throwing water kegs in every direction, they ran for their lives. I rode up alongside of the hindmost squaw and shot her dead with my flintlock and called to "Eagle Head" to take her clothes and scalp. The man who was mounted escaped to camp, but the nine squaws were all killed. That was not all – we were hardly through when we discovered over a bank quite close to us a great crowd of squaws also getting water – who had been hidden from us by the high bank. To these we turned, and a massacre followed; not a woman escaped, although, there must have been a hundred there. I did not kill any more, but contented myself with riding around and heading off and driving back any who were getting away. When the last squaw was dead and scalped we started for home. The Crees were soon in hot pursuit; we went slow, allowed them to catch up to us then turned and charged them, killing their leader. We retreated, the Crees followed, and we turned to charge a second time but they gave up the fight and went home to their dead wives. Home was reached in two days. There was great jubilation in our camps, especially amongst the Sarcees.

"Wears his head ornament behind" was the name of the leader of a rather large war-party which started from our camp on Bear River. At Dirty River one day, during a fall of snow, some of our men thought that they saw a herd of elk. I brought my glass into use and made out their elk to be a travelling camp of one lodge, but many horses. We followed their tracks and when close to where they camped two men went ahead, stole some of their horses, and at once set out for home. A man of the strangers came over a hill nearby driving the herd of horses. Our party, thinking that it was a crowd of mounted Indians, turned and stampeded. I saw what it was and went towards the herd to get a shot at the one herder, who saw me and retreated towards the lodge just as I was about to fire at him. He threw himself from his horse and slipped over a small cut bank and escaped. I caught his animal, mounted and drove away the fine herd of horses. I drove on and passed my companions, who were strung out in a long line, just as they had fled, the fastest runners being the farthest away. Each, as I passed, asked me for a horse, but I appeared not to hear nor see them and drove my horses right on past them all. Then I waited and gave each a horse as he came up. There was a mount for each one and many to spare. On the way home we over-took the two who had taken the first horses. The snow was so deep that most of the animals played out before we reached home.

At Fort Benton I met and joined a very large party of Blackfeet who were going on a war expedition to the same favorite place, the country of the Crows. Running Rabbit was chief, one called the Gambler and I were the only two Bloods in the party. Somewhere about the locality where I had taken the horses on the last trip, we passed an immense war-party of Crows. The two parties did not pass in sight of each other, but were some distance apart, one going North and the other, us, going South. The following day we saw their trail and our leaders decided to let it go and push on South. At about the same time the Crows crossed our tracks and turned and followed us for two days. They kept us in sight without our knowing it and they let us travel on into their country until a suitable spot was reached for their purpose. While going through a very rocky locality we discovered that every stone rock and bush ahead of us was hiding a Crow Indian.

Running Rabbit had told off three to go and scout in front, Rough Head, Flying White Buffalo and I. The other two had gone before me and when I caught up to them they were lying on the edge of a hill and closely examining the land ahead. I had taken out my glass, but found it of no use just then and laid it down beside me. At that moment Flying White Buffalo called, "We are chased – we are chased," and sure enough behind us, between us and our company, was a great pack of Crows coming towards us. Fortunately between them and us was a big coulee which was full of soft snow and impassable. We ran around the head of the company and fell into another one. By the time we extricated ourselves the Crows were close upon us. One of the Blackfeet with me was nimble and got away. The other was running behind me, when he stopped and told me that he was shot and I went back. This prevented further running on his part but he managed to walk. The bullets were flying thick about us and I was anxious to use my legs, but the wounded man begged me not to leave him and I could not refuse his wish. I walked with him and helped him along as fast as I could. Again my companion was shot this time through the hips and of course he had to sit down on the ground, no more walking was possible for him. He still prayed to me not to desert him and there I remained in his vicinity, dodging here and there to avoid the flying missiles. How I did long to try a race with those bullets. Our foes were now up to us. One short black-faced fellow, took courage at the sight of the wounded man, and came running up to him. The latter fired at the Crow but missed and the gun was wrenched out of his hand in an instant and up came a number of our enemies who seemed to pile themselves right onto the wounded Blackfoot. I rushed at them and fired a shot amongst them which scattered them in all directions. Our men now arrived and we chased the others away. They retreated past the place where they had been in ambush for us and I, seeing a fancy gun cover standing up against a tree ran to it, thinking that I had a gun sure. But I was not so lucky. It was only the cover, inside of which were those two little long sticks that Indians use as a rest in hunting. All were now engaged in a running fight with the retreating Crows. We shot one of them through the arm cutting an artery, the man fainted just as some of the Blackfoot, reached him; he was quickly deprived of his scalp, arrows, and coat. Our adversary next found good cover, and made a stand and from every tree and rock they were firing at us. They had chosen the situation well, for at the time they ceased their retreat we were in the open and quite unprotected. We were forced to fall back to cover ourselves and that made the distance so great that the fighting was harmless. Before we retreated we killed another Crow, but could not get at the body, so procured neither arms nor scalp. The Crows, though vastly in the majority, now signalled to us to go home, and we made similar signs to them. When we returned to our Blackfoot wounded man, he was dead; we buried him where his body could not be found, hiding it under a pile of stones. We went home via Fort Benton and to camp on Sun River. Although bringing back arms captured in war and a scalp there was no rejoicing, for we had lost one of our party. Spring was about to break when we reached home.

After a short rest I led a small party of Bloods upon a trip to the Crow country. We found on our way many stray horses that had been ridden down and left behind by different war expeditions, and taking possession of these we returned homeward. At Fort Benton I met my uncle "Far Seer" and was told by him that a great expedition was about to leave against the Snakes, who had lately killed some of our tribe. I told my relative that I would be one of the followers of "Sun White Buffalo," for it was he who was to lead.

The Bloods were at that time camped along the Missouri far above Fort Benton and were moving down to the place where they always procured their supply of red earth. The exact location of the camp was given to me and leaving my companions I pushed on, being afraid of the war-party starting before I arrived. When I reached the place there was nothing but a deserted camp-ground. I had only taken enough provisions to last me to that place, so was now obliged to search about the camp ground for scraps of meat, enough of which I found to do one. I followed the broad trail and finally reached the camp which was across the Missouri.

I was disappointed to hear that "Sun White Buffalo" and the band of young men had been gone two days. There were other small camps of our people up the river in several different places, "Sun White Buffalo's" own lodge was at one of the most upper of these small camps, he had only come down to the main camp to get a following for his trip. I procured from my friends and relatives a supply of moccasins and, after eating one hearty meal, I started the same day that I arrived to overtake the others. Their path laid up the Missouri and that night I slept at one of the upper camps. Early next morning I was up and following the many foot marks of the war party.

Before the Sun was high I arrived at "Sun White Buffalo's" lodge and his people informed me that the ones I was following had been gone three nights. I now knew that unless I did good walking for a few days I would be too late.

The trail was plain and I at once set out upon it and travelled all the rest of that day and well into the night without a pause, I laid down and slept at the spot on the prairie where I happened to be when I felt so inclined and was up and going before the Sun next morning. That day I found some dried meat at one of the camping places of those in front of me, which I acquired and ate. On I went at my best gait and did more walking than sleeping that night, and at the close of the following day I overtook the expedition just after they had built their shelters and were almost to repose. I had only been out 2 nights on their trail which had taken them 5 to make, of course that was because they were many and not in a hurry, while I was alone and very anxious.

When across the "Elk River," a small group of us left the main party and took an easternly direction. We discovered the trail of some "Crows" and followed it up and took all their horses, some of which were good large ones. For home we rode, and found our village on Bear River. I was very sorry that I had parted with the main party for when we got in, they were there before us; they had found a small camp of Snakes which they had completely annihilated and captured all sort of goods, some horses and the much-prized weapons. Our camp moved to a place called "wide bush" near "Snow Mountains" and from here I started upon my next war-path.

This was a few men only under one known as "Carries Tail Feathers upon the Hill." Near the "Elk," while I was out scouting with another fellow, I saw two horses which I caught. They were probably stray animals. One of them, a black, I gave to my companion, the other I presented to our leader, who, now having what he came for, at once turned and went home in company with another who rode the black which had again changed hands. Leaderless, the rest of us continued our search for adventure. At a Mountain known as the "Owls Bars" we found a camp of Crows. At night we went to their horses but could not catch a single one although we tried all night to do so. They were fat and mean and would not let us close to them. While we were in cover next day the camp moved away and, some of us being tired, we returned home to camp, which was on the Yellowstone. One night only was I at home.

Next day while I was up on a hill looking about and resting I saw what looked like a small war-party which sneaked out of camp and went off in the directions of the mountains. I went to my lodge, gathered up some moccasins, my rope, etc., end ran after and overtook them. They were, as I expected, on the war-path under the "Martin." We went over the Mountain to the vicinity of a trading post there and climbed a timbered mountain and camped where we could see over a great extent of country. We saw two riders driving horses from the North. I watched them with my glass and noticed that they rode like drunken men this was because they had been driving day and night and were sleepy. They had no doubt stolen the horses from our country and were now on their way home. Thinking that they would be easily ambushed in their sleepy condition, I and another went down to kill them and re-capture the horses. We reached a point directly in front of them and sat in the bushes in wait for their approach. Soon they were close to us, when the leading horses seeing us shied and ran back. The drivers rounded them up and started them on again but passed us at some distance out of gun range so we returned to our friends empty-handed.

Again from our high position we saw an enemy, this time it was a single horseman coming from the distant trading post. To make sure of him we all descended and hid ourselves in a line across his path to prevent a repetition of the other escape. Presently he appeared riding out of the bushes in front of where I and some others were. The "Martin" told me that he would kill the man and that I might take the gun. I was not in an agreeable humour for I fired first myself and killed, the rider, calling to a young relative of mine, who came and took the gun. A Piegan of our party took the horse. The man we killed was a good looking fellow, with very long hair; he had a new white blanket tied behind his saddle, no doubt he had just bought it. We then went home rejoicing and at the Sweetgrass hills we found camp on the move Northwards. It was early one morning when we overtook the travelling camp. My relatives had stopped to hear my story and had given me some food which I was eating as I sat on the ground. While thus occupied we heard that some Crees had been seen in front of the outfit, and by the time I had procured a horse a man rode from the front saying that the leading people were fighting. I put whip to my horse and soon left the women and horses behind, there was no difficulty in following the fighting people for the way was marked by a string of bags and other heavy articles which the Bloods had cast from their horses as they galloped after the Crees. Soon I passed a wounded man who had been shot through the hips and there I saw our fleeing enemies going out of sight over a hill. I was riding a big bay horse, a present to my uncle from Culbertson. As he was fast, I took what I thought a short cut to head off the Crees but they did not go in my direction and I missed them altogether.

When I Joined the rest of the men they had given up the chase, having killed one Cree who was scalped before I saw him. All returned to the women. When we camped that night there was plenty of fun for the merry makers. Two victories had to be celebrated, two scalps to be danced for, which being taken from enemies of different tribes and under such different circumstances, the cause of joy were multiplied, here was little or no sleep to be had that night.

Once, when I was a mere lad, I was permitted to go with a large war-party under the Chief "One Spotted Horse." The Crows had been stealing our horses and this expedition started from our main camp at a place below Fort Benton, to retaliate. At the Elk River was a trading post frequented by the Crows.

We arrived in that locality and from our hiding places saw large numbers of that people camped about the Post. Other lodges were continually coming in and camping there to trade. One Spot considered that there was going to be serious work and called the party. A large party like that always has men in it, who though being either too old or too young, are liable to tire and be a nuisance to the good men. The ground there was very muddy and travelling was most tiresome work so our leader ordered most of the men home, some old, others young fellows amongst the latter myself. But I and two others made up our minds not to go and said so. The Chief at first explained that none could remain but the stronger and most experienced. Finding persuasion useless, he abused us and called us all sorts of nasty names for our disobedience. We did not mind the abuse as long as they did nothing worse, so stuck to them and followed wherever they went. The culling out had cut us down to only three brush lodges. We three boys were punished in many ways for not doing as we were told. A buffalo was killed and we were forced to pack nearly the whole carcass. We were continually carrying water to the men and whenever they would catch one of us sitting down, they would find some errand to keep us busy. They thought that they could make us tire of their company, but we took all in silence and remained. During the stay there, a rocky place on a hill was fixed up as a fort to retreat to in case we should be hard pressed in any trouble that might follow, and near this hill beside a creek was our brush camp. Early next morning some of the men were up on the hill, looking at the surrounding country, when they saw a great crowd of Crow Indians coming straight towards our camp. Of course they thought that we were discovered, but it soon turned out that it was only a buffalo hunt, for one of them chased an animal and killed it and his example was followed by others. Their reason in turning out so early was, the muddy ground in the morning was stiffened with frost and buffalo were more easily run than would be the case later in the day when the heat of the sun had thawed it out. It was still early in the day when the hunters finished their work and returned to their village. All this time we three boys were kept in a hole and told all sorts of lies about what was going on. When the Crows had all gone out of sight, our men descended to our brush camp and all prepared for action by painting up, etc. We boys were told to paint our faces and go off by ourselves and take horses. That no men would be allowed to accompany us. In fact we three were treated like stray pups following a camp. No one had a pleasant word for us, nothing but offensive torments and insults were bestowed upon us. But to all such, we simply sat and in perfect silence, acted as if we heard nothing.

We all approached the Crow village and found that it was a large one stretching far up the river and down, so we went into cover where we were to wait for night to come. All about the different groups of lodges were playing crowds of young people. Long hours we waited until the Sun began to sink and finally the people transferred their merriment to the inside of the lodges. At last the welcome darkness enveloped the scene and our time for action had arrived. The chief first told a certain tall man of the party to go and take a scout by himself, and to do it very cautiously. This was a mild way of telling the fellow to go and take the first chance at the Crow horses. One Spot pitied him, probably because he was poor and wanted him to be successful. The tall person, went as he was told, and took the hint also, for he came back in a short time with three horses. The chief sent him to the fort with his animals, the rest of the party were now told to scatter and for each to act according to his Judgement. Our leader said, "There are the horses before you and their owners asleep." Away we all went, some up the rivers, others down, and in a little while the village of the slumbering Crows was being approached from all directions.

I and one other boy went together up-stream and picked out a group of lodges. We were crawling along through the grass and bushes, close to the lodges, when we heard something behind us and presently saw that it was another of our men upon the same errand as ourselves. We could see that he did not know of our being here so we called him to us and found that it was one called "High Sun," my brother's companion, who then offered to stay with us and lead us, he being much older than us. "High Sun" led the way far around and closer to the lodges which we saw were pitched in a circle around a corral in which the horses were. Our companion told us to remain there and he would go ahead and see how things were situated. He took his departure and we could see his form as he boldly walked between the lodges and approached the corral. We waited a long while, then he returned and gave us a spear which he had captured; we could not see it plainly but between seeing and feeling we could tell that it was richly ornamented and a valuable trophy. High Sun at once went back again and next time brought with him a big grey horse, and told us to leave the place and go with him to our retreat. We all started away, but I and my friend soon stopped and told the elder one that he had got all he wished for but we had nothing and were going to get at least some small article each before we went hone. High Sun exchanged his rifle for his young brothers bow and arrows and parted with us. We returned to the place we had just come from and took the same path between the lodges that High Sun had. The corral was full of horses, and my companion wanted to go in and take some of them. But I had noticed a hut of shields and other articles hanging on the usual tripods near some of the lodges and I preferred then to horses. So like fools, we stood there and argued about it in whispers. Finally we parted, I to the tripods and he to the horses. At the first lodge I took from a high tripod, which I was obliged to lower to reach the articles, a shield and some bags of Indian goods. in front of this lodge, which was a large one, was tied a horse which soon I untied and led away, his color I could not make out in the darkness. Another lodge I went to, and found that against it was leaning another tripod also supporting a shield and some bags. It was not such an easy task to remove these articles as others. Leaning, as they were, right against the lodge, the least sound or clumsy movement would awaken the inmates. But I was cautious and not in a hurry, so made no noise.

I spread my robe upon the horse's back and tied each pair of bags together and slung them over the horse, the two shields I put on my back with their streps around my neck. I discovered another horse, also tied near a lodge, and led them both away from the camp. I was obliged to go very slow, for all the stuff I had was covered with bells, and would make an uproar at the least quick movement of the horse. I went near to the corral and found that my friend had gone. After slowly walking the horses out of earshot of their late owners, mounted the one with the bags etc. on and directed his steps towards our fort, leading the other. All was well until I had reached quite a distance from the Crow lodges. The horse I was riding then became inpatient to return home, and when he found that I would not allow him to, he began to pound and dance up and down. Of course the bells all made a row and the two shields on my back rattled together so loudly that the horse became more unmanageable each minute until finally down went his head and I was bucked off.

I did not let go of the bridle but the animal I was leading got away from me when I fell, and back home he galloped at his top speed. Being afraid to mount, I led my horse away far out on the prairie, until I grew tired of walking and again ventured upon his back. Now, however, he had recovered from his uneasiness and gave me no more trouble. I was still out at daybreak, then for the first time I saw that my horse was a fine buckskin. As I neared the fort my stud again began to dance, and in that style I went in, the horse prancing sideways, showing first one side then the other to the watchers on the hill, my goods with many bells jingling in time to the horse's movements. When I saw the black looks of envy upon the faces of the warriors I felt amply revenged upon them for all the insults I had suffered at their hands. I tied up my horse and unloaded my captures, the men all came around, and we turned out the contents of the bags. Everyone admired the number and quality of my trophies. In one pair of the bags was a man's suit complete, shirt, leggings, etc., all of the very finest of an Indian Chief's ornamented clothing. Those bags contained much more than we Bloods put in them, the Crows seemed to keep all of their finery there. There were even beads and women's trinkets in one of them. I was soon plied with many requests from the men for this article and that. Most of the things I gave them, reserving for myself the shields and some of the best of the other. One of the shields was a beauty, it was fringed with eagle tail feathers and red cloth. On the front was painted a mountain lion, there was a bullet hole through it and blood all over the inside. The strap was a band made by doubling a whole deer skin over and over. I now had time to enquire about the fortunes of my companions. Only a few of them had been successful. The Crow horses were too securely corralled for many of the oldest of the party to take. The spear taken by High Sun and which I had handled in the dark, I afterwards examined. It was one of the best spears that I have ever seen. The handle was covered with buckskin and decorated with crows feathers. To it was tied a stuffed crow's head, which the owner was wont to tie in his hair before going to war.

Next night under cover of darkness we left our hiding place and started upon our home journey. After many days we arrived at Fort Benton, and then came up home, to the Blood camp on Belly River.

From the Bear River where our camp was situated, a party started under the joint leadership of White Wolf and myself. One day, after we had arrived at a point below the trading post of the Crows, I saw some buffalo and took out my spy-glass to examine them. Upon looking through it, I discovered a horse-man who was in the act of ascending a small hill. He remained but a short time on the hill, going there no doubt to observe what direction the buffalo were travelling, after which he descended and went out of sight behind some ridge or high ground near him. While still looking in that direction I saw a large number of people appear from where the rider went to and attack the buffalo. From our hiding place we watched the runners kill many animals, butcher and carry away the meat, but could not locate the village. At night, however, we left cover and had no trouble in finding the camp, which we watched until its inmates were asleep. I divided the party in two; one half I took charge of, the other was under my friend White Wolf.

I and my party at once set out for the opposite side of the camp. Upon our arrival there I found that the village was pitched upon an island, formed by the river and a slough. The latter was dry and the rocky bed of it was all that was between us and the hostile camp. Prom where we stood we could plainly see that our enemies' horses were loose in the camp, and I took one young man with me and a Blackfeet and, telling the rest to remain where they were, led my companion quietly towards the village. I did not cross on the stony bed of the slough, for it is not easy to walk over stones without making some noise. At one end of the slough was a patch of still back-water from the river and this patch was frozen over, it being late in the fall of the year. Upon this ice we crossed noiselessly and were soon nearing the camp. As I was about to lead the way between two lodges, I heard my young companion whisper from behind something about "a person" and "a log." Casting my eyes quickly about me I saw no person but a large log was quite near me, a fallen tree. My companion repeated his warning, and I now saw that it was no false alarm, for right close to me I could see the figure of a man lying flat beside the log, no doubt a guard over the horses. As I looked at him he slowly arose to his feet, gun in hand, which he cocked as he reached an upright attitude. My gun was already cocked and ready for instant use, and there we stood looking at each other for some little time. My friend had fled when the Crow stood up, so I was quite alone in an interesting situation. Without taking our eyes from each other for an instant, the Crow and I slowly began to back away from each other. My adversary backed towards the nearest lodge and as soon as he reached its immediate locality he, with a spring, got behind it and took to his heels and was soon out of hearing. As soon as I saw this trick I turned and soon put a good distance between myself and such a dangerous neighbourhood. Upon reaching the place where I had left my party, I found that they had taken fright and stampeded, but I listened and heard their distant retreating footfalls. I started in the direction of the sound at my top speed and when about to overtake them, one of them saw me and yelled, "here comes a mounted man," at which they scattered in the darkness like so many birds and I would have been left alone had I not called to them. When they heard my voice they ceased their wild race and I got them all together again.

Knowing that nothing could be done in the way of capturing horses that night, we went away from the locality of the Crow camp. In the meantime, the leader of the other squad had heard talking and moving about in the village and surmised that there had been a discovery and had retreated to the open prairie and took the same direction that we did. One of my boys saw the outline of their figures against the sky on a hill close to us. Thinking of course of enemies instead of friends he gave the alarm, said that we were pursued, and it was with difficulty that I prevented them from stampeding again. To make sure, I quietly approached the travelling party until I was close enough to hear their voices, which I recognized as those of our other party. At the same time that I became thus satisfied of their identity they saw me and scampered off like rabbits, but I called after them with the effect that our two parties were soon reunited. We at once continued on to the brush lodges where we had spent the night before, and after we had rested a little while, I proposed that we start out for fresh fields as it was still a long time before daylight and we could go a long distance that night. White Wolf would not listen to that, he said, "we have done these people no harm yet and some of their horses will be ours before we leave this vicinity." After long and useless argument I said, "Stay here and attempt the Crow horses if you will, but I am going away in search of a new village, for I am satisfied that no good will come of roaming about the neighbourhood of people who have discovered us." I called upon a young relative of mine to come with me, and he and I packed up our bundles and were soon ready to start. I went out, but when he got up to follow me the others took hold of him and said he should not accompany me. I demanded his release, but found that every man was opposed to me, upon this I gave in saying, "All right, here we shall stay and tomorrow the Crows will find us and we will suffer; you will all have cause to regret this foolishness."

Early next morning I went in search of a better place to defend ourselves in, should we be tracked and attacked. A suitable spot was up above us in the hills and they all followed me to it. Here we remained that day without seeing anyone, but in the middle of the afternoon they took a sudden notion to start. I objected to this very strongly, for I thought that we were watched by our enemies, all had been so quiet that day. Another reason why I felt cautious that day was this: the crow birds were sitting on the trees near us all day long, that I knew to be a bad sign. I took it as a warning and tried to control my friends. I said: "What fools you are, you refuse to move at night but want to do so next day in broad daylight. No; No; here we must stay until night."

They were all of one mind, however, and start they did. I, of course, was obliged to go too, but I scolded them much as we went. I said, "Oh you fools, you are going to catch it this day." We entered a long coulee and started down it to where it would emerge upon a river bottom. As we neared the mouth of the coulee, an elk was seen, and one of the crazy men would have shot it in spite of my opposition had I not used deception to prevent him. I volunteered to shoot the elk myself, and crawled towards as if to do so, but I showed myself purposely to the animal which scampered off. I was obliged to lie to my companions and tell them how I had endeavored to get a shot at the elk. Later on I played a similar trick with a buffalo bull to prevent the men firing at him. Towards sun-down three more buffalo were seen and they all said that they were determined to have meat. They fired two shots and killed one of the animals which they set about cutting up.

Four of the men went off to take a scout around, and I went to the top of a hill in the vicinity and sat down. Three other men sat with me, the others were all busy with the meat. We were all hungry, but not enough to take such a risk as we were doing. They called to me to join them, but I preferred to remain where I was. I felt an uncontrollable presentiment of coming evil and in

36

obedience to it I spent my time in overhauling my bow and arrows and examining my flint lock. While all were thus occupied, from my positions on the hill I saw a great horde of mounted Crow Indians coming in sight from the coulees and other favorable places that had enabled them to approach us. They quickly formed in a solid line, in which form they came towards us at a gallop. I called to our men below "Come up here! Come up here! I am not going to run, I am not going to run." But they were panic-stricken and ran about in all directions and were easily run down by the Crows, who had seven of them dispatched in as many minutes. These were the leader "White Wolf," "Gambler," "Singing Back," "Many Gifts to the Sun," - Bloods, and "Good young man," "Many Tail Feathers," and another fellow, whose name I do not remember, Blackfeet. One only, a Blackfeet, managed to reach us on the hill, this made our number five. We ran for our lives, hoping to reach some friendly cover. We kept together and did not get at all excited, although we knew how very slim our chances were. Soon I heard a great yell behind me and saw that a Crow mounted on a big bay horse and armed with a spear and a shield was about to run me down and spear me. I put an arrow to my bow and as my pursuer came upon me I turned and let it go. He was coming at such a speed that I missed him but the arrow was buried to the feathers in the horse's kidneys. The horse bucked off the rider, who fell on one side, his spear on the other, while the shield rolled away over the prairie.

This did not detain me a moment but on, on, we flew, and another Crow got after me. He was mounted on a buckskin and held in his hand a gun with which he intended to shoot me. I waited as before until he was almost up to me then I turned and shot an arrow well aimed for him. I made the same error, as I fired be turned his animal sideways and the arrow struck the horse in the same place as the former had, and down came the Crow to the ground. We had now retreated a long distance from the starting-place and one of my friends called out, "a coulee! a coulee!" and to my delight right in front of us was a coulee, into which we ran and hid in the brush in the bottom. We were doomed to be disappointed in the matter of cover, for we soon found that it would not be of any use to us, it was so scant. The Crows were on both sides shooting down upon us and soon would have killed some of our now small party had we remained there. I told my friends that we must break out of that trap and up we went, up the opposite bank, through the yelling Crows and off across the level prairie, our pursuers shooting at us all the time but keeping a good distance away. Soon a welcome sound came to our ears, a repeated and echoed two yells which I had found by experience to be the Crow signal to cease fighting, which they did at once our nearest pursuers contenting themselves with a parting shout and a shot.

During our retreat homewards that night we overtook our four men who had gone scouting. They had heard the firing and yelling and had at once fled thinking it certain that they would be the only survivors of the party. We nine continued homewards, and at Fort Benton met the first of our people and related the story of the misfortune. The news did not reach the Blackfeet camp until the following Summer. While we were at Fort Benton we were surprised and glad to welcome a strange arrival. He was no less than one of the seven whom we thought, dead, away down in the Crow country. It was the young Blackfoot whose name I do not remember, he told us how he had been badly wounded and when the Crows were busy elsewhere he had crawled away unnoticed into slight cover and thus had remained until night-fall. In the pursuit of my companions and myself nine of us were hit; but for my part, I know that many a bullet hole in my garments told me how near I came to finding a bed on the prairie. In this run the Crows captured six scalps, the arms of six men and three black-covered medicine pipes. Of the four scouts who were away and thus escaped, Old White Wolf, the blind man now on the Blood reserve, is one; he was not then called by that name.

I was a member of a large party which made an unsuccessful trip to the Southern country. Returning homewards in the month of December, at Fort Benton we met a small party of Blackfeet going South. I and four others joined them. We went down to the mouth of the Sun River, where was situated the Gros Ventres camp, and here we were obliged to walk some days. The Missouri was full of floating slush ice and we had to wait until it was frozen over. We at last crossed and away South we journeyed led by the Blackfoot, "Big Road." We crossed the Elk River and neared the scene of the affair with the Crow in which we had lost six men. This was near a placed called by us "Lonely Mountain." We had seen no buffalo since leaving the Missouri and our stock of meat was very low. Arriving at "Lonely Mount" we saw three buffalo, one of which I managed to kill, a bull, very fat like a young cow. We cut up the meat and carried all we wished with us. Not far away was a good camping place, which had been prepared by a party of Bloods upon a former trip in which I had taken part. To this I advised my friends to go, as there were plenty of brush lodges ready, made as well as a good strong fort with large logs piled up all around, 3 high. To this place we went and occupied the lodges. As the weather was cold and there was a little snow upon the ground, some of the men went and trapped coyotes, the skins made them good warm beds to lie upon.

The day after we arrived at this place one of our men, while out trapping, saw a long line of Indians carefully following in our tracks of yesterday. We were cooking and eating when this man ran in with a frightened face and related what he had seen. We were not allowed much time to make ready, for we were at once surrounded by yelling Crows, who at the first volley broke the leg of one of our men and the arm of another, the former was Weasel Horse, the latter was a Piegan Medicine Shield. On one side of our enclosure stood a large tree, and upon one of its branches was hanging a black-covered medicine pipe. Soon after the attack one of the Crow made a bold run upon the breastwork and secured the pipe. He was quick enough to regain this ground unhurt with his prize, but had no sooner done so than he was grappled by another Crow who wanted to take from him his trophy. There they struggled for the pipe right before us but I settled the dispute, for I took aim and while they were so engaged and shot one of them through the back, he fell like a dead man. The enemy made a great fix and for a long time they amused themselves by throwing fire brands at us, no doubt hoping to burn us out, but that did us no harm for all that came inside we extinguished. At another time one of them crawled in towards us and fastened a rope to one of our logs and they all pulled on the other end, thinking to haul away our barrier and put us at their mercy. Fortunately the rope broke and we were safe again.

All this time a continual shouting and yelling was kept up by both sides, each man of us had his place in the enclosure, and as I laid flat in my corner a bullet struck the log near me and a splinter of wood struck me in the forehead and cut a deep gash. The blood from this covered my face and as I was too busy to rub it off, I soon was a bad sight to look at. My comrades inquired what was the matter, and I replied that I "had almost been wounded" I still bear the scar from that splinter, it is large and plainly visible over my left eye.

I do not consider that I was wounded by the Crow, for his bullet did not touch me, as this was the only time in my life that my blood flowed in battle. I still boast that no enemy has ever struck or wounded me. The nearest man to me was a Blackfoot, who was badly wounded. He was struck in the middle of the forehead by a bullet which cut a gash in his skull about two inches long, we thought that he was killed but he came to just before daylight next morning. Long in the night I saw a group of Crow about a fire. I took a shot at one of them and knocked him down. The others got away from the fire. I do not know where he was hit, but I afterwards saw much blood at the place where he fell. During the night the enemy recovered the body of the man I had killed near us. One of them crept up and fastened the end of a long rope to the body and others in cover hauled him in. We took possession of his bag and contents as trophies. During the progress of the fight we were asked what people we were, and we replied, "Blackfeet, Bloods and Piegans." At noon we saw the Crow leave in a long line for their home; for miles they were in sight winding over hills and at last they were all out of sight. We left our retreat and scattered over the battle-ground, examining the signs, when from cover we were fired upon by a large squad of the Crow that had been left there to ambush us. We regained our fort and did not leave it for two days more, but contented ourselves with doctoring the wounded, resting, cooking and feeding up for future possibilities. The fight lasted from four o'clock in the evening until noon the next day. I never heard that we had killed any but the two I shot and we only had three wounded. We supplied the man with a crutch, who was crippled in the leg, and on the evening of the third day we started out upon our return northwards. We took care to camp every time in a strong position and did not allow our stock of meat to get low.

One night, while we were engaged in cooking and eating inside of our barricade, I heard plainly a crack as of a twig or stick being trod upon, we looked at each other and exchanged whispered opinions. Nearly all of us had heard the noise, so we dropped down behind our cover, with guns in our hands. I called aloud, "Somebody in this locality will get hurt before long," and to our great surprise a reply came out of the darkness in our language, "Don't hurt me, Don't shoot us" and in came two men, Piegans. They had been of a war party of their own people and had became separated while on a scout. They told us that they had seen us killing buffalo and had watched where we camped, but could not tell what our tribe was until they heard my warning. They remained with us and we continued our way homewards until across the Elk River. Here eight of us turned back on a new war-path, not caring to go home as things were. We headed to the Red Mountain and discovered a camp of Crow. One night while scouting near this camp one of our men discovered something which sent him to us in alarm.

Others went to see what it was but upon their rejoining us we were no wiser than before, for they seemed to have no idea what they had seen, except that they had seen something. I thought that it must be the carcass of a horse or colt and went to examine the object. What was my feelings to find that it was the stripped and mutilated body of a man, we afterwards heard that it was the body of a Blackfoot who was one of a war-party which had met and fought the Crow.

On the following night we went close to the Crow village and saw that they were having a scalp-dance. One man was singing and a crowd of girls were dancing. We crawled in close to the lodges and laid where we could see and hear all that was going on. One of the girls called out in our language every little while some such expressions as "My friends go away, you will be killed" or "My friends you are watched." I remember that these repeated warnings had a great affect upon the younger members of my party, who wanted to take the girls at their word and go home at once. I had some difficulty in reassuring then that these girls were captured women taken from the Piegans from time to time and that they were no doubt in the habit of calling out such warnings when they felt like it, and that no doubt the affair in which the man we had seen, had been killed in, was why they were so noisy tonight. When the dancing ceased later on in the night, and the people had all gone to sleep, I and a Piegan went in between the lodges and approached the horses. The latter looked very queer in the darkness, my companion declared to me that each horse had a man on its back, and as they looked that way to me we were upon the point of stampeding in consequence. We mustered up enough courage to go closer and make sure, and then we saw that the light had deceived us, the horses were unguarded. We each caught and mounted one, and quietly and slowly drove a large herd of the animals out of the camp and away to our waiting friends. All were soon mounted, and away we flew to the North. Elk River we crossed near its mouth and our camp we found on Bear River. I had many horses to give to my relatives this trip. The Blackfeet who was shot in the head in the early part of this expedition, lived for many years after the receipt of the wound. He had always warned his wives that if they eat buffalo feet, his wound would get bad and kill him. Some years afterwards they became careless and neglected the warning, by having a meal of buffalo feet. The result was what the man had predicted, his head swelled up and he died. His name was "Crow on side of a butte" Mas-tau- ac-a-kip.

"Big Road" was leader of a large party of Blackfeet and Bloods who went from the camp at Bear River. The object was as usual Crow horses and I of course was one of the party. Soon after we crossed the Elk River we saw some Crow hunters where we tracked to their camp, and as usual laid in cover until the inmates of the lodges were wrapt in slumber. A warm wind had been blowing all day, thawing away the snow that was on the ground to the thickness of an inch or so. At the moment that we had concluded the village to be securely asleep, the wind shifted to the north and a bad blizzard set in instantaneously and howled about us in a perfect fury. We lost no time thinking about the storm, but scattered out around the Crow camp to see what could be obtained in the way of horses. We crossed the River which was before us and I and two Blackfeet, "Bad dried meat" and another, went in the circle and found the horses were all inside a strong fence or corral and caught one of the animals which were standing with their backs to the storm. My two companions did likewise, while I caught and bridled a sound animal for myself. I hunted about and found a weak place in the fence. We lifted a log and took it from under a stump that supported it, then let the log to the ground; the horses I then led over this log to the outside. The upper log was Just high enough to enable the horses to pass under by slightly bending their backs. When my companions had both passed out with their horses, we broke into a run and recrossed the river, the ice was covered with water from the late Chinook and by the time that we reached the top of the bank our moccasins were frozen stiff. We mounted and sped away in the face of the blinding storm. When we had placed a safe distance between us and the village we dismounted and led our animals to keep ourselves warm, in this way we travelled some distance. One of my friends, who was not warmly clad, showed signs of freezing and to prevent that misfortune, we halted in a timbered coulee and built a fire to warm him. I and the others changed moccasins and after I had stuffed the cold mans clothes full of grass, so full that he could not walk without difficulty, we took the road again, walking in the direction the still furious storm came from, and leading our horses. At times when the ground was favorable we would run. We descended another bank and found ourselves at a creek, near which was no timber but heavy sage brush. We made another short halt, built a fire, thawed out again and continued our way. We saw nothing but ourselves all that night until after daylight next morning the storm cleared away. "Snow Mountain" and "Black Mountain" were in sight and their positions showed us that we had travelled straight northwards all through the storm. We arrived at the Southern Bear River and there killed a buffalo and had a feast of ribs, etc., and slept in an old brush lodge we found. On the following day we pushed on and the chinook again began to blow, making the ground muddy to such an extent that one of our horses played out and we were obliged to remain and rest him. Next day we started again and I went on ahead, walking, the other two following with the four horses. I happened to look behind once and saw that there were only three horses, so waited until they caught up to me, then enquired what had became of the fourth. They had stuck a knife in him because he could not keep up with the others.

We arrived at Fort Benton and went on homewards. This was a very quick trip. Five days afterwards our main party came into Fort Benton and related that they had taken some horses, had been discovered, had retreated, and in the storms they had lost one of their men through being frozen to death. They also told that we three were lost, probably dead, but they were informed that we had passed safely home five days ago.

"Big Road" and his comrade "War Bonnet" led the following expedition. It was not a large party and we had a long way to go, because our home at that time was camped away north at the edge of the Northern timber and our object was as before Crow horses. The berries were beginning to ripen as we completed our preparations and went on directly to "Red Mountain" which we climbed for the purpose of viewing the country. One morning I and another were out upon a scout and while going up a coulee we were suddenly confronted by a bunch of buffalo who looked at us in a startled manner. In an instant the side of the coulee was swarming with Crow Indians in pursuit of the buffalo. We popped into what bush there was at hand and were fortunate in being able to do so without being seen. From our hiding-place we saw a Crow having a rough fight with a buffalo bull which he finally killed. While the rest of the buffalo were being hunted, a bull came panting along and laid down to rest beside us. Our brush cover was not all dense and we viewed this newcomer with dismay, for bulls in that hunted tired state are very hostile and he might see us and attack us. Again, the Crow were liable to come for him and find us. One by one the hunters finished their work and rode away over the hills with their meat. Our bull companion watched them attentively and at sundown he too got up and took his departure, to our relief. We descended the coulee, and by keeping in a long strip of heavy brush, we made our way very quickly and safely to our companions. They had in the meantime built a good place to retreat to in case of trouble and as soon as we related our little adventure all made ready to take action. We took the direction that the Crow hunters had, and there found a creek which we followed to a lately deserted camp-ground. This showed us that the camp had moved directly upon the return of the buffalo hunters. When engaged in going over the ground, as Indians always do, we suddenly discovered one large painted lodge standing alone. This was a puzzler at this, and when after a consultation we went close and looked inside.

It was only to find that the lodge was quite empty. We afterwards learned that it was a Crow religious custom to make a sacrifice of a good lodge to the Sun, in that way. A chief upon buying or making a new lodge would sometime leave the old one standing where it was last used. We left the locality and ascended a big hill some miles away. Here we waited until daylight, thinking that we would then see where the Crow had gone to. We were right, the camp was plainly visible in the distance, and we rested all day waiting for the friendly darkness to come. We left our high hiding-place at nightfall and approached the village which was situated upon a burnt piece of prairie. We were divided into two parties, which took opposite sides of the camp. I was told by the leader of my squad to take one man and go into the village and drive out a herd of the horses. He thought probably that I was a fool that would walk into a hostile camp and drive away the horses as if they were my own, and I at home!

I said nothing, but called one of the men and went; we stopped outside of the lodges. The horses were loose and were slowly wandering out to graze. After a large number were some distance clear of the village, we got up and drove them away to our waiting friends. My companions caught a bay on the way and mounted him. Soon the men were all busy amongst the horses looking out what to catch. Then a great blunder was made; some fool caught a wild horse, and although a number of the men ran at once and helped him hold it, the animal got loose and ran through the herd with the long rope about his heels and legs which ended in a wild stampede back to the village. All was commotion in the camp, and we could hear the people driving picket pins to secure the animals. They no doubt misunderstood the excitement of the horses, I thought, so proposed to make another trial. Many of the men wanted to go home. Three times I enquired who would come with me for horses, but there was no response, so off I went alone. Near one of the lodges I heard a woman crying, and to that point I directed my steps. I walked boldly towards and past the woman and as she did not notice me I coughed when opposite her. She turned and watched me as I stalked past her, my arms hidden under my blanket-coat which was pulled tightly about me. She renewed her crying and I passed between two lodges into the middle space. I put my rope on a pinto mare, but when I attempted to lead her away, she would not come and then I saw that she had a great swollen knee. I turned her loose and caught another mare and, avoiding the crying woman, I led her away out on the prairie, tied her to a bush and returned to the camp. At the back of a big lodge were a lot of bags, etc., tied to a pole which was leaning against the lodge. This I tried to unfasten, but could not succeed. In the dark I could not see what the bags were fastened to and, while reaching up in my attempts to untie them, the pole slipped and the whole affair came down with a crash, me on top of them. Hearing a noise, as of some sleeper getting up inside the lodge I quickly put an arrow to my bow and moved to the entrance of the lodge, determined to shoot any one who might come out. A few grunts, however, told me that there was no fear of that and I returned to the bags and took them and walked away, dragging the pole after me. I had not gone far before I was spoken to from behind. Not knowing the tongue was of course I could not reply, but when a second remark was addressed to me by my follower I took to my heels and ran away, still keeping my goods, I reached my horse, got rid of the pole and mounted. I rode towards the lower end of the camp and saw three men whom I took to be of our party and addressed them. They did not reply but, laid low in the grass. As they were quite near enough to hear me, I knew them to be Crow, and turned my horse away. The mare was a fast one, and well for me that she was, for in response to yells of the three Crows, the women in the village set up a great uproar and immediately the whole neighbourhood became alive with mounted men yelling and running in every direction. Without a doubt the camp had been on the alert and its inmates waiting for us ever since the horses stampeded home. I found myself closely pressed in the darkness and threw away my bags to help the little mare. A shield on back was the only article I retained of my new captures. My pursuers were well mounted, and I was soon overtaken and headed off. As a last resort I threw the shield away and urged my mare to her utmost. Away we flew in the black night, my escort yelling like mad men, and I with only a few yards start. A coulee lay before me, and with a bound I was at the bottom of it and quick as thought, I turned my horse's head up the coulee without slackening speed.

The trick saved my life, I think. My enemies bounded up the opposite bank of the coulee and away then went in search of me on the prairie in that direction. I struck into a patch of timbers at the head of the coulee and then halted in good cover. Before long I heard some riders come up the way I had, and as they passed my hiding place my mare attempted to neigh. She would have betrayed me had I not struck her on the head with my whip. The searchers passed away in the darkness and in the distance I heard a gun shot, another, then many shouts and yells and a continued shooting, after which there was comparative quietness. I left my cover and again went towards the camp, where a great fire was burning and crowds of people seemed to be moving around it. I had a notion to creep in and take a shot at one of those people but changed my mind and instead retreated to the meeting place of the war-party, where I arrived after daylight. My friends had given me up as killed. The shooting that I heard was caused by the discovery and death of one our men, one of those who had gone to the lower end of the camp. Had they not found and killed him they would probably have given me a longer chase. Some of the other men had been successful in the matter of horses and all started at once for home. On our way North we struck the Piegan camp and as they could tell us nothing as to the whereabouts of the Blood camp, we remained with them. The mare I kept for myself. Many of her colts and her descendants are in my band yet.

"Wolf Chief" was the leader of this war-party, which was a large one starting from our village on Red Deer river (north). At the Sweet Grass Hills we found the Piegan camp.

This trip was my third to the Red Mountain country. South we travelled, and Just before we reached the country of the Crow, we met a single Blood Indian coming home with two horses he had taken from these people. He had lost the rest of his party at night and now turned and went back with us. This man and three others rode the two horses. The rest of us followed as rapidly as we could. It was night, and suddenly we saw the flash of many guns ahead of us. Our four men we thought were in trouble, or at least discovered. The four we did not see, we retreated knowing that nothing could be done there. The Red Mountain we climbed in the dark and there passed the night.

After daylight one of our men noticed an object upon a distant hill, which he thought to be a person. Others of us differed from him, thinking the object to be a crow-bird. While we were watching and discussing the black mark a long line of horsemen came in sight on top of that same hill, and then we found for the first time that two of our men were not with us. They had fallen behind in the darkness and had slept by themselves away down the Mountain. It was towards them the Crow were going, they had not discovered us. We all ran down to help our men, and from rocks and trees held back the Crow. They evidently thought us too strong for them, for two riders were dispatched to camp, as we guessed for more help. There was a young Blood with the Crow, he had been captured when a child, as his parents were out hunting. This youth called to us in our own language enquiring who we were. We told him some of our names. He named many of his relatives and asked if they were alive. Some of them were in our party and we told him so and asked him to come over to us, that we would not hurt him. He seemed agreeable and came closer once, but turned again saying that he would get his horse. We decided that if he came, we would force him to stay, but would do him no harm.

Soon he returned with two others whom he left some distance away and advanced alone riding a buckskin pinto with black ears. Before he had quite reached us he halted, as if afraid to come to us, then a relation of his, one of our men, went out and met him. Our man enquired of him if he was armed, and he replied that he was not; the other then went a little closer but was afraid to go right up to him. Then they stood a few yards apart, afraid of each other. All the time the two Crows kept calling the young Blood to come back. He told us that if we had lots of ammunition we would require it, as reinforcements were on the way from the camp, which was a triple one composed of Crow, Snake and Nez Perce Indians. The Crow camp alone, he said, was very large and from such a number of lodges there would be a great crowd of men. "Do your best! Do your best!" said he, "the people from the three camps are going to make it hot for you."

After giving us this encouraging news, he turned and re-joined the other Crow. Long before this we saw the Crow turn loose their horses to graze and now we could see them sitting on a hill waving their hands to us to go home. In reply we only waved to them to do likewise. We busied ourselves making our position stronger. It was already good, but we rolled plenty of big stones in place and otherwise improved it. Near sundown the Crow on the hill began to move about and through my glass I saw them all saddling up and leaving the spot. Down near to us they came, shouting that they were going home and telling us to do so too. They had not seen anything of the expected reinforcements and were not inclined to attack us alone.

They all passed out of sight, but had no sooner done so than, from the same direction, we saw approaching some horsemen, whom we at first thought to be our four men that we had lost the night before. In ones and twos mounted men came in sight until the hill was black with people, then we understood how matters were. The retreating Crow had met the reinforcements and now we were going to catch it. One man rode far ahead of the others; he wore a hat, a buckskin shirt and had an American flag wrapped about his body. He was riding a buckskin pacer; he rode up to within speaking distance of us and called out, "My friend! My friend! I am a Nez Perce, I am a Nez Perce." He then rode up to within twenty paces of us, dismounted and deliberately let go his horse and drove it away with his whip. This seemed to be a signal, for at once a great charge was made upon our stronghold. Mounted and yelling men were upon us in every direction. Some of our party were stationed out a little distance around us, hidden in holes and behind rocks.

The enemy rode right in between these out-pickets and the rest of us. I fired a shot, missed my man and while in the act of loading my flintlock I turned and saw behind me a man on a blue roan horse. On his head was a horned war-bonnet streaming away out behind him. He carried a shield, and an American flag was tied about his person. My chum and I had agreed not to empty our guns at the same time, but in turns. Therefore his gun being now loaded he fired and brought down the wearer of the fancy clothes. I ran forward to capture the trophies, but the man who was only wounded, got up before I reached him and made his escape. Some now at the same time made a rush at me and tried to cut me off from my companions. But I got back to my place all right. Someone called me by name to go and take possession of a shield and spear that were lying beside the body of a man he had just killed. I looked about but could not see any dead man, and again he called to me a second and a third time. I replied, "There are others nearer to the body than I am, let some of them make the captures." At last I jumped to my feet, saw the articles mentioned, made a dash for them just as their owner crawled to the edge of a little bank and rolled over it and out of sight. The spear and shield I secured, and had I been a minute sooner the Crow would have lost more than them. In the midst of a storm of arrows and bullets I regained my position.

All the Crow near us seemed to have fired at me. There was a lull in the battle after that, they all retreated to a distance, probably to have

51

a talk. One of them then showed himself upon a neighbouring hill and signed to us to go home. We, as before, made the same signal to him. They only wanted us to leave our position so that they could charge us in the open. I gave our chief "Wolf Chief" all the things I had taken. At sundown the Crows all went out of sight. At dark our leader proposed to start for home, but I would not agree. I thought that we ought to do something more before we left the locality and said so.

Our party split into two, half with "Wolf Chief" went home, most of the younger men were in that band. The older and better men all remained with me to seek fresh adventures. We left our late battle-ground, and I led my men away around to the country on the opposite side of the Crow village, where we arrived at daylight. We heard shots in the direction of our late retreat, and with the aid of my glass I saw the Indians running buffalo. Their camp was in sight of us. Four days we remained in hiding and then the village moved and was pitched right near us. There were many buffalo about there and the Indians were busy all day killing and taking in meat. I was suffering much with rheumatism and said: "To-night I will accomplish something or get killed, in the latter case my limbs will pain me no more." So at night we filed down the hill and noiselessly approached the camp. It was moonlight, and some of the Crow were parading in their village, which was an immense one, singing and calling out at intervals. Several times they shouted out in the Blackfoot tongue: "My friends, beware; My friend go away – Do not come closer." These remarks had a bad affect upon some of my comrades who wanted to turn about at once and go home. I lost patience with them and said: "All right, you all go home, leave me alone to do the work." I took off my leggings, prepared to act and asked who was going to follow me. No answer, I enquired again and a Piegan named the "Lazy Boy" volunteered to come. I told the others to go to a certain place and wait for us.

The Piegan and I waited a long time. A cloud darkened up the moon and caused a little rain to fall, the singers went into their lodges and long afterwards the horses began to stray out of the circle, grazing. My companion thought that he could distinguish riders amongst them, but it was only his imagination. I roped a black and the Piegan a gray. We drove away a big herd to where the rest were waiting and then all were soon engaged at the pleasant task of catching horses to ride home upon. We drove away our new property and a snow storm came up.

We went around the mountain and ascended the other side and at our late battle-ground we camped, keeping the horses well out of sight in the timber. All the next day we watched the excited Crow, a large party of whom went North in pursuit of us. They never guessed that we were looking down upon them from their mountain. Next night we set out for home, but we took the precaution to make a great half circle towards the North, the straight line we left to our pursuers. We saw no Crow or other hostiles on the way home. Winter had set in when we reached our Blood camp which was pitched on Stand-off bottom.

The Bloods were camped at the Red Deer and a number of our horses were stolen by the Cree, although we were at peace with them at the time. I led a war-party of seven men to see what we could do in the way of retaliation. The Cree were bad Indians, who deserved to be punished. They were not honest, they stole horses. Yes they did, they were horse thieves. We being mounted made fast time and going in a North-easterly direction, saw in the distance a big blue hill looming up and near it a large Indian camp. Between us and the camp the country was very level so that it was not safe to travel any closer in daylight. During our waiting hours that day I went upon top of a hill with my glass to see what might be in sight. I saw a few lodge poles stuck up in the shape of a lodge.

After examining them a minute I looked in another direction and saw a large war-party coming along and heading in the direction of the lodge-poles. My companions signalled to me to come down and eat as they had been cooking. I watched the war-party, until they took up the trail of the people who left the lodge-poles and followed it out of sight, then I went down and had my dinner. Upon returning to my station on the hill, what did I see but a single tall man following up the trail of the war party, this individual appeared to be unarmed. I ran to my horse, mounted, and followed by my companion, galloped after the lonely man. We reached him just as he was down, drinking from a little rivulet or spring. I was on the lead and dismounted and seized him as he arose to his feet. I searched him for arms, but nothing did I find. The man was poor, he had not even a knife. I was so disgusted that I left him to the boys, to do as they liked with. One said to kill him. I did not like Cree Indians well enough to say no, I said nothing. As there were no arms to take I did not say, "kill him." The end of the matter was, this, I blackened his face, praying to the Sun as I did so, and gave him to the Sun unhurt as a present. When I told him that he was free and might go he looked very much surprised. But he did not wait for us to change our minds, but walked rapidly a few yards then broke and ran like a deer until out of sight. I guess he had never heard of one of his people falling into the hands of the Bloods and living to tell about it. No doubt, if living, he wonders yet to what good circumstances he owes his really remarkable escape. I do not think that he would ever guess the truth, that, he was not worth killing!

That night we set out and rode all night long. At daylight we were close to the village and continued towards it. The people saw us and came out in a big crowd, one mounted man enquired who we were and was told, at which he returned to the village. We rode right into the camp and the Indians had a big talk, likely were Assinaboins, but the lately arrived war-party were Cree. We saw our tall friend again, who was relating to his people his adventure of yesterday. It appeared that they all called him a liar and then some came to me and asked if what the tall fellow said was true. I, of course, told then it was. A chief told me that I had a very strong heart, to turn loose a man like that unhurt. We remained there two days. The war party had a dance on the second day and two of us went to see it, although we were warned by a friendly Assiniboin not to go near the dancers or they would kill us. They had a very fine dance, their war bonnets, shields, etc., were good, but the dancers acted in a queer manner. They would come near us and point their guns at us in a nasty way. Between dances they, counted coups, which all seemed to be about Bloods, Blackfeet and Piegans! One of them spoke in our language. He named a Blood that he had killed, he described the horse the dead man rode, and which he captured. This was too much for my good temper. I got mad at once, peeled out my knife and walked into the circle shouting - "You are no good! – You are no good!" I then began to sing and yell and count coups against them. I told them that I had killed three Cree in one day. It was a lie on my part, but I was an eyewitness of the event that I referred to, so was able to discuss it to their satisfaction. They thought I spoke truly. I only wanted to make them angry because they had succeeded in making me so. I told them lots of lies about Cree that had killed, scalped, and taken guns from, and the women all began leaving the camp, taking their children away to the bush. On a pole in the dancing circle was an H.B.C. flag and on the ground beside it was a bow and thirty arrows. A man stood by the flag pole. I went, and with a yell cut loose the flag and took possession of the bow and arrows. Then, turning my back upon the Cree dancers I told them once more that they were no good and stalked away with their flag etc. When we entered the lodge of our Assiniboin host he informed us that some of the Cree war-party had been trying to bribe him to give up our horses to them. This news made me more hostile than before. I called aloud to the Cree to bring out all their warriors and fight us seven Bloods, but my challenge was unheeded.

Shortly after that we started for home, the flag I presented to my chum, "Big Plume." Two incidents occurred while we were in the hostile village. During the first day, we were all sitting in our host's lodge when an old man entered with a big knife in his hand and sat down near the entrance. Seeing him casting sundry bad looks at me I asked him what he was after. He replied: "You have eaten four of my children — Four of my children have you eaten!" He was probably referring to four of his sons killed some time in the past while on horse-stealing expeditions in our country, so I replied, "What are you talking about? Did I tell your sons to come and steal my horses. Did I ask them to come away down there and get killed?" The old fellow no doubt saw the truth of my argument for he did not make any attempt to use the big knife on any one but went away soon. On the day of the dance, in the morning, we were sitting in front of the lodge and saw an Indian with his face end hair all plastered with mud, which also filled his ears. His arrows were turned wrong end up in the quiver and he was using a rattle and singing beside a hill. Wandering about in that manner he came across a pot full of meat which he fell upon and devoured. Then he renewed his run and went over the hill. Our host explained that the fellow always acted that way when hungry.

A large party started from the Blood camp on "Cut Bank." The leader was "Running Rabbit"; the destination the Crow country. At Sun River all turned back but three, myself and two others. On our way South I found six stray horses which we were satisfied with so turned and came home. Our village had by this time moved to Fort Whoop-up, and when we reached them we found camped the Blackfeet, Piegans and Sarcees in addition to our own tribe. The Blackfeet chief, "Sun Old Man" was about to lead a large mounted party against the Cree, in the North. I joined the party.

I gave away all horses taken on the last trip and borrowed from my relation his fastest horse to ride on this war expedition. Away up on the Saskatchewan we saw a fleet of thirty boats going down the river. The white men landed on our side and we sat in a big circle and received many presents. There were three principal chiefs in our party who took the goods and distributed them to all.

The white man told us that the gifts were to encourage us to trade with them. Blankets, tobacco and goods of all kinds were given to us. In return some of the men took off their fancy dress and presented them to the chiefs of the boat people. The boats floated on down the river and we continued our search for Cree villages. For a long time we sent out scouts with no success until we met a small party of our people returning homewards with Cree horses which they had just stolen. These men gave us the location of a hostile camp, to which we went. The Cree were wide awake. Their lodges were pitched on a level prairie with no brush or hills near enough for us to approach unseen. Some of us proposed to play buffalo and draw the Crees away from their lodges. Others wanted to ride boldly up and attack the camp. The latter plan was the one followed. We walked our horses directly towards the camp making no noise and showing no haste. Some Crees saw us and fired at us but we walked right on, paying no attention to them. Then but a short distance from the village we charged it. Men, women and children fled like coyotes. Some of the men were posted out about the camp behind blankets and robes but they also fled at our approach.

I cut a big slit in a large lodge and jumped in through it to see what I could capture. All I got was a bag of sundry goods and an axe. I went out, remounted, and off to see how things were going on. My uncle "Far Seer" saw a man coming out of a lodge and rode up and shot him dead. We afterwards learned that it was a chief named "Handsome man." A great many more Crees were ran down and killed. We lost three of our own men. One was shot in the head and killed. Another was shot by an arrow, in the head, we tried to pull out the arrow, but it parted with the point, which remained in the skull. That man died two days afterwards. Our leaders having ordered us to fall back from the camp we did so. One of our men wearing a war-bonnet rode back alone to the camp to attempt some brave action and was killed. Many others were wounded by the Cree arrows. All the bodies of killed and wounded were taken away by us. We had a good supply of scalps and trophies of all kinds and started for home when the fight was over.

The Blood camp was moving South to the Sweet Grass Hills and a long way ahead of us at Blue Lake was pitched the village of the Piegans. A war party of nine Crees stole horses from the Piegans and retreated with them northward in the direction of Cypress Hills. The Crees did not know that the Blood camp was in front of them or they probably would have taken another road. It was early one frosty and foggy morning in the early fall of the year. We had been all out running buffalo. I had returned and entered my lodge, leaving my buffalo horse, a very fine one, tied at the entrance. Some riders dashed into camp with the news that nine Crees were passing on their way north with Piegan horses. All was then in an uproar. I at once went and caught another fast horse which I mounted to save my racer, which I led. Seven of the pursuing Piegans came in and then a crowd of us went after the thieving Crees. "Far Seer" took the lead.

We had no difficulty in finding the trail of those we were after, for it was plainly to be seen in the white frost-covered grass. Beside the tracks we came to a carcass with a buffalo chip burning on the ground. We guessed that they had halted there to smoke and had knocked out the contents of their pipe on the buffalo chip which had afterwards caught fire. Farther on we found another sign of their smoking. The pursuers divided, "Calf Shirt" took one half and started direct to Cypress Hills to cut off the Crees. "Far Seer" with other men continued on the trail. The fog had now lifted, I changed horses and with five companions went off to one side. I told my uncle to watch me all the time, for if I saw anything I would signal to him. We had not gone far before we got amongst a herd of buffalo and near a prairie lake I saw horses grazing with the buffalo. We went back a little way and got behind a butte and obtained a better view. All we could see at first was the horses, and one man busy skinning a buffalo. We flashed a glass at the nearest of "Far Seer's" men, who were disappearing in hollow ground, but they did not see the flash. I saw away behind a single horseman

58

and flashed my glass at him. He pulled up at once and I flashed again, at which he started after "Far Seer" at a great speed and I knew that they would soon all be with us.

We now went down and approached the lake and there were sleeping eight men, the ninth, the one butchering, got up to his feet. He was a boy, he saw us and called to his companions in alarm. Up they jumped to their feet. I wanted to go at them but my friends the Piegans with me, held my bridle saying: "Wait, take no risks." The Crees were mounted and away in a minute. Then the Piegans let me go and away I pursued the Crees over the prairie. They had a good start, but I saw plainly before me the nine horsemen. One of the horses ridden by the Cree was not fast enough, but its rider got off and mounted behind one of the others. Then that animal, thus double laden, began to fall behind the rest. I was now far in front of my friends and rapidly closing up the gap between the two laggards, when the leading Cree reached a coulee, dismounted, and turned to help the two I was chasing. It was now my turn to run, which I did, and not any too soon, for a gun or two was fired at me as I flew out of range. My horse being tired, I dismounted to rest him and wait until the men arrived. The Piegans soon came on and a fight started. The Crees called us all sorts of nasty names in bad Blackfoot. My horse, having regained his wind, I went around to the far side of the enemies' coulee. Our main party came along and as the nine doomed men saw their number they killed their eight horses for a barricade and dug their hole deeper. The battle now began in earnest. We attacked them on foot. Whenever they showed an arm or head before firing we did not retreat but simply dropped flat in the grass. In that manner we slowly closed in upon them in a circle and at last made a rush and finished the affair in a hand to hand struggle, in which the nine Cree were killed. They wounded many of us, but none seriously. The fight lasted longer than you would think from my story for our charge was made after sun-down and we went home in the dark. I took some of the captured articles but did not kill any of the dead, for I had no gun. "Big Snake" got one gun, "Many spotted horses" another, and some Blood took the third. That was all the guns the Cree had. Upon our return to camp all the people painted their faces black and we had a gala time because it was a complete victory.

The following took place when I was young. It was the third trip under "Red Old Man." Our camp, from which we started, was situated on the Two Medicine River near its mouth. It was in the fall of the year. Our trail led away to Fort Benton, then South across Elk River, where there was a trading post frequented by the Crow. We did not call at this post, because the white men there did not like us, they were in the habit of shouting at us whenever we gave them a chance. So, keeping clear of this dangerous place, we passed on to Lonely Mountains.

When we reached that locality a heavy fall of snow came which left the ground covered to quite a depth. A Crow village was found, the inmates of which were not at all on the alert. They doubtless thought that there was no danger of war-parties being out in such deep snow. Their horses were all grazing outside of the camp, a fire-place and many foot marks showed us where the Indian boys had herded horses and played during the daytime. We could not catch the animals very well where they were, so drove them off to the river above the camp. At a watering hole was a sheet of glassy ice and onto it I drove some of the horses. I roped a big black-eared gelding and got on his back while he was on the ice, but as soon as he reached the shore he bucked us off into a snow bank, and got away with my rope on him. Five were still on the ice, and I hastened back to them. There was one there that I was sure was gentle and to it I turned my attention. Having now no rope it was by no means an easy task to secure him. Every time he tried to run off the ice I grabbed him by the tail and jerked him and about. Finally, I headed him in that manner to a big snow bank at the edge of the ice and as he entered it I sprang upon his back. Away we flew after the herd which my friends were driving away. I was quite at the mercy of the horse I rode, and hung on with all my strength by its mane. The men stopped the herd and I dismounted and caught the one with my rope on. To see if he was really unbroken I again mounted, but was promptly bucked off. That satisfied me, and I took off my rope and caught and rode the other. I rounded in the four that were still on the ice and now having acquired six I was ready to leave the vicinity. All that night and all next day we drove at a fast rate of speed for home. During the day we crossed a trail of a war-party, a large one going north. We rested the second night and in our front we saw a camp-fire. Some of the boys thought it a star, and four of them went to see which were right and they returned and said that it was a star. Next morning we soon found our mistake, for in front of us was the tail end of a war party so large that the leaders were not to be seen. The Crows, for such they were, spread out on each side in order to prevent us from passing. Away to one side was a ridge with a bare strip on its side where the snow had been blown off. We headed for the near end of the ridge, and upon gaining the low ground we made our horses go at such a speed that our unmounted pursuers were soon left far behind. One little colt was left behind in the snow and was caught by the Crows. In this band of horses were two mules, one a bob-tailed and split-eared animal was given to Culbertson by "Red Old Man." The Blood camp we found on Sun river. I was armed with bow and arrows only in those days. "Long Hair" now living in the upper camp, was one of that party.

"Not a Favorite Child" was the leader. From our camp on Sun River we went to the lodges of the Crows that were pitched on Stinking River. This was a place where the Crow often made their winter camps. It was a hard place to take horses from, for the reason that it was in the middle of a perfectly level prairie which was too wide to be crossed twice in one night.

I mean that a war-party, that waited until nightfall before they started to walk across the prairie, could not reach the camp, capture horses, and get out of sight again, before daylight, so wide and level was the plain about Stinking River. The Crows had there constructed permanent corrals which they used year after year. These enclosures were very well made, strong and close. So close were they built that horses on the inside could not be seen from the outside, and moreover all sorts of thorny bushes were used in the construction, making it nasty work for any one who tried to tear them down. In times of very deep snow I have known the Crows to cut young cotton trees down and feed them to their horses, which would eat the bark and thrive as well as they now do on oats. We saw that there was a camp on the river and late in the afternoon we struck boldly across the plain, unseen, and at dark were not far from the village. When we went close to examine the lay of the land we discovered a fresh difficulty. The wily Crowe had picked out a most strong position. The village was nearly surrounded by the river which then made a bend of almost a circle. in the circle was built the horse corrals, and besides them were pitched the lodges. At the narrow neck of land leading into this circle some boys were building a fire, so that it was impossible to pass out that way with horses.

The river was covered from bank to bank with a sheet of most slippery glare ice. You see what difficult work lay before us. We had our choice – go home on foot, or get those horses. It was decided that none but the older and most experienced men should go near the village. When they had departed upon their dangerous errand, one called "Spotted Wolf" enquired who would follow him. No one answered until he had asked the question a third time, when I said, "Go on, I will follow you." I was both young and foolish then and had no right to go, but he wanted a companion. "Spotted Wolf" was a great walker. He started off at such a pace that I had to trot to keep him in sight. He stalked straight towards the place where the boys were building the fire, and although it was getting dangerously light there, we managed to crawl past on the dim side unseen.

Near the fire a number of young men and boys were sitting, a guard I suppose, in charge of the horses. We reached the corral, got inside, and after a lot of trouble succeeded in making a hole big enough for a horse to pass out of. We then each caught a horse and led him outside, which we had no sooner done than we heard a great row at one of the other corrals. One of our men, a blundering fool, had entered that corral and caught a mare with a bell on her neck. He attempted to lead her out of a place where she would have to make a high jump to get through. The mare tried it but fell back making a row with her bell that roused the village in an instant. Many of them ran to the narrow place and cut off that means of our escape. Then the women began throwing burning sticks on the ice so that their husbands could see to shoot. I and my friend at the first yell sprang upon our horses and jumped them onto the ice nearest to us. My animal was sure footed and after many slips and much struggling carried me to the other side in safety. Looking back I saw that my comrade was not so fortunate, for his horse was down. My first impulse was to let him shift for himself but I changed my mind, dismounted, tied my horse to a tree, and ran back on the ice. I pulled the horse by the tail, "Spotted Wolf" pulled him by the rope on his neck, and thus we slid the animal over the slippery Ice to the edge, where he quickly gained his feet. We mounted, and not an instant too soon, for the Crow had seen our actions and were almost upon us. Away we galloped with a shower of arrows and bullets after us. Our chief had taken out a horse from one of the corrals before the row occurred, but no others than we three did. One called "Many Strikes" obtained the trimming of a wax shield, but not the shield. The fellow who caused all the row carried away the mare's bell, which he had taken off and put over his shoulder when he saw the mistake he had made. My capture was a bald-face bay.

I led a mounted party of seven to Cypress Hills. One day, while on the North side of the hills, we turned loose our horses near a spring and while one man on a butte kept watch the rest of us took our meal below. While busy eating, our lookout called to us, "Here comes a rider quite close." We saddled up, and the man on the hill kept telling us where the stranger was, but he did not turn his head once towards us for the others would have known then that he was not alone and would have escaped. The stranger, a Cree, took our friend for another single Cree, and rode right towards him. At last he rode in sight and we all galloped out, surrounded and captured him. I took his gun and told him that he could go unhurt. As he went at once I guess he is still rustling grub somewhere.

While at camp on the Red Deer, a party of Blackfeet went down the South Branch of the Saskatchewan and captured some Cree horses. Upon their return, they informed the camp that the Cree were only a few lodges that could easily be wiped out. Accordingly a large party was organized and went down to perform that always pleasant task, under the leadership of Weasel Horse. Instead of the expedition returning in triumph with many trophies of war in the shape of scalps, guns, horses, etc., a few only came in, the survivors of the war-party who had found many more Crees than they were in search of and had been nearly wiped out themselves in consequence. A great council was held to decide what steps were to be taken in retaliation. The result of the "talk" was that the Bloods, Blackfeet, Piegans, and Sarcees moved in a single immense camp down the river. A war-camp of the whole nation upon an errand of vengeance. When we had moved a long way down the river, one day "White Calf" and "Eagle Head" with a few men went out upon a scouting trip. After they had been gone two or three days, early one morning they appeared in sight, riding in circles and as they approached we saw that they were flourishing a scalp. They had discovered a Cree village and at some little distance from it came upon a man and a woman. The former made his escape, but the woman, who was heavy with child, fell into the hands of the scouts who soon despatched her. The news spread rapidly through the camp, and soon in all directions were to be seen the men catching and saddling their war-horses. A great war-dance was indulged in by the mounted men until all were ready, then off they started, hundreds and hundreds in number, a fine sight. As the Cree camp was not far from ours, our scouts were able to note the size, shape and position of it before sundown. It was a large circular camp, situated on the open prairie. After dark we went in close and took up a position in a large coulee quite near the camp. It then began to rain and did not clear up until daylight. We made ready to strike as soon as there was light enough. In the camp amongst the lodges were a lot of hobbled horses, which were first of all untied and driven away to a safe distance by our men. The noise aroused the slumbering Cree and in a few seconds all was alarm amongst them. The women and children quit camp and flew to the timber. The men at once opened up a fierce fire upon us. Our leaders ordered us to retreat slowly away out on to the open plain, so that the Crees would follow and enable us to charge. We fell back from the village, the Crees pressing in pursuit. When a sufficiently long distance was between them and their camp, we at a signal, turned and went at them. They did not attempt to make a stand but fled in the wildest disorder, and were slaughtered like buffalo. I rode after three Crees, who turned to meet me. One had a gun, two were armed with bows and arrows; the latter shot many arrows at me as I went towards them, then they turned and ran away. Their companion with the gun waited for me to get quite close, he evidently intended to make sure of me. On I rode, straight for him, and at last when almost upon him, he fired and missed me. It was his last shot on earth for although he bravely clubbed his empty gun to strike me, he fell in an instant with my bullet in his breast.

The gun was taken by a young relative of mine. I picked up a fine robe with a chief's coups painted upon it. We again started away as if to retreat and a number of Cree fools mounted and came yelling after us. Again we turned and drove them back. Our people would ride alongside of them and catching them by the feet would throw them from their horses. A Blackfoot chased one Cree, who was so thoroughly frightened that he soiled his horse's back. The man was killed, and the horse taken by the Blackfeet. The only casualty on our side was one young "Blood" killed.

We now returned to our lodges. "Calf Shirt," father of the killed boy, waived the mourning custom in this case. He said: "Be joyful; do not mourn for my son, you have killed many enemies and captured much." So in great glee our camps were moved back to our own country.

"Red Old Man" was leader of a party who left for the Crow country from our camp on Bear River. At the "Owls Ears Mountain" a Crow camp we saw on the move, which we watched and noted the place where they pitched for the night. The moon was at the full that night, and "White Buffalo" and I went together to take horses. We did not for a long time go near the camp. Some of our men had that day done some shooting before we saw the Crows, and I was afraid that the latter had heard them so was more cautious than usual. When it was late enough for the Crow camp to be slumbering and no signs of any of them being about, we crept in close to the village, the lodges of which were showing plainly in the bright moonlight. I was in favor of waiting for horses to come out to graze, as they nearly always do before morning, but my companion was impatient and we went in. We followed down a little creek and saw the horses all in open ground out of the village, one lodge only standing near them. We approached the horses. Between us and them was a pile of drift-wood amongst it a big fallen tree. I was almost up to that log when I saw a face appear above it, and knew at once that I was in a trap. It did not take me long to see my only chance, for I no sooner saw the face than I turned and ran away at my top speed. A shower of bullets was fired at me but none hit me. The Crows came yelling after me, I had not a long start, but I did not need one. I was so scared that I seemed to fly over the ground. A cut-bank laid in front of me, in the moonlight I could not tell how steep it was, but went at it and was surprised to find how soon I reached the top. I ran onwards, heard my name called, altered my course towards the voice, and met my friend and with him ran into a slight hollow, the only cover near. The mounted Crows nearly rode over me several times. My heart thumped loudly at such times and I grasped firmly my gun, resolved to kill at least one man before I fell when discovered. But the Crows did not see us. When in this anxious situation I made a discovery that scared me more than ever – my powder horn had been shattered to pieces by a bullet and I had no powder. When the Crows fired at me from the log, I was so interested in my speed that I did not notice that one bullet hit my powder horn. While thinking over this misfortune a cloud obscured the moon and we quit our place and ran for the nearest ridge, and reached the other side in safety before the cloud passed away and it became light. We continued our flight for some hours and then had a sleep. Upon awakening in the morning, we found that we were not alone: for near us quietly sat a wolf. My friend, at first proposed to kill him but I said: "No, let him alone." That wolf followed us all the way home. At night time he would sit nearby and howl. During the day he kept close at our heels. We killed buffalo whenever we were hungry, and our friend the wolf contented himself with the entrails only. At last the Piegan camp was in our front and there, in sight of the lodges, the wolf left us. In camp our relatives had all given us up for dead, the other members of the party had gone in, before us and reported us killed.

These are the principal adventures of my life, about which I am not in the habit of talking, for I am not a boaster. Only upon a few occasions when I lost my temper have I said that I was strong. All the people know me, and my doings. I have had enough war and trouble in my time and know what it is. That is why I try of late years to keep the young men quiet, they do not know what they say when they talk of war.

I was never struck by enemy in my life, with bullet, arrow axe, spear, or knife!

(End of Red Crowds Biography)

Made in United States
Troutdale, OR
08/01/2023

11726105R00043